Christ and the Sacrament Church

Michael Witczak
8. VII. 1963

Pierre Talec

Christ and the Sacrament Church

Translated from the French by
Joachim Neugroschel

The Seabury Press / New York

SAINT FRANCIS SEMINARY
St. Francis, Wisconsin

To my mother, to my father,
the roots of my faith.

1983
The Seabury Press
815 Second Avenue
New York, N.Y. 10017

Originally published in one volume
as *Les Choses de la Foi: Croire à l'essentiel.*
Copyright © 1973 Éditions du Centurion, Paris.
This is the second of two volumes.

Library of Congress Cataloging in Publication Data
Talec, Pierre.
    Christ and the sacrament church.
    Translation of: Les choses de la foi.
    "Originally published in one volume as Les choses
de la foi: croire à l'essentiel . . . This is the second
of two volumes "—T.p. verso.
    The first volume of the English translation has title:
Jesus and the hunger for things unknown.
    1. Jesus Christ—Person and offices. 2. Christian
life—Catholic authors. I. Title.
BT202.T3713   1983   232   82–16842
ISBN 0-8164-2455-1

Peut-être que j'ai faim de choses inconnues.
Perhaps I hunger for things unknown.
Valéry Larbaud

"I know whom I have believed."
2 Timothy 1:12

Contents

Christ and the
Sacrament Church

1

Jesus: Someone Full of Life

The Resurrection I

Now if Christ raised from the dead is what has been preached, how can some of you say that there is no resurrection of the dead? If there is no resurrection of the dead, Christ himself cannot have been raised, and if Christ has not been raised then our preaching is in vain and your faith is in vain; indeed, we are shown up as witnesses who have committed perjury before God, because we swore in evidence before God that he had raised Christ to life. For if the dead are not raised, Christ has not been raised. And, what is more serious, all who have died in Christ have perished. If our hope in Christ has been for this life only, we are the most unfortunate of all people.

But Christ has in fact been raised from the dead, the first fruits of all who have fallen asleep.

(I Corinthians 15:12–20).

"If Christ has not been resurrected, then our faith is in vain." These are St. Paul's words. He spoke them to the Christian community in Corinth (I Corinthians 15:14–19). The Church today cannot better that statement!

"If Christ has not been resurrected, then our faith is in vain." Clearly, this affirmation resounds with the provocative assurance of a priori statements that are always right. Who could, who would dare think the contrary?

"If Christ has not been resurrected, then our faith is in vain." For generations, Christians have been repeating this first and obvious fact, rooted in them by centuries of Christian experience: If Jesus the Son of God is not resurrected, then he is dead for all time. If God is dead, God is not God. If God is not God, what is faith in God? Imperturbable as this logic may be, it does not, however, condemn the Christian to accept the resurrection as strict dogma.

· **Christ, Our Will to Be**
If Our Life Is in Vain, Then Our Faith Is in Vain.

Christ's doctrine is not a set of dogmatic statements. Every baptized person is asked to verify personally by the particular experience of his own life, the universal truth manifested by baptism: Christ is our resurrection. By living this experience of faith, in the heart of human realities shared with all human beings, the Christian, existentially speaking, can no longer accept distortion between the things of life and the things of faith. The things of faith are the things of life lived in the light of Jesus Christ. The Resurrected is Jesus Christ, our will to be. The resurrection is the fundamental fact of faith, because it is the fundamental fact of life. That is why if our life is in vain, then our faith is in vain. The resurrection assures us that Someone is full of life. Has always been full of life. Will always be full of life. Full of life for today. Full of life for each one of us. "If Christ has not been resurrected, then our *faith* is in vain." All we have to do is replace the word *faith* with *life* to hear the same cry: "If Christ has not been resurrected, then our *life* is in vain."

The resurrection challenges every human being. It raises the question of the meaning of life for each one of us. It presents it as a choice to make, a direction to follow. From the moment we believe that life will always be life our daily life changes. As Simone de Beauvoir speaks about growing old in *Force des Choses*, we can submit ourselves negatively to old age and think of it as decrepitude, the road to nothingness, or positively, and think of it as the road from one life to another, a trying passage, to be sure, but nevertheless a way of being.

The Resurrection, a Struggle for Life

If Christians are truly convinced Christians, they are convinced above all of the triumph of life. If God can't die, then life can only live. This Christian hope goes beyond Christians, because it is each and every one of us who is called to live by Christ, the life force. Thus, Christians can no longer regard Christ's resurrection as solely concerning the baptized. Ultimately, the resurrection is the only news that interests the world every morning. If today, many nonbelievers wonder about Christ's resurrection, it's because they more aptly perceive the crux of the issue—perhaps through the questions that Christians ask themselves. Our question of faith challenges their lives.

The resurrection is at the center of all the questions a man may ask himself about the meaning of his personal existence as well as the meaning of the world. If there were no resurrection, the struggle for life would probably be no more important for human beings than for beasts in the jungle. Man cannot accept the idea that life ends in nothingness. The resurrection—whatever one's interpretation of the word—reveals that it is contrary to nature to admit the end of everything. Death cannot have the last word. Whether by way of political action or any action for a more humane society, the resurrection is always the motive for this life force. That's why Christians and non-Christians must understand the questions asked by others as their own questions. The dialogue between the believer and the non-believer is not a friendly get-together with each side tolerating the other; it is mutual recognition of the same questions asked differently by each side.

The Straw and the North Wind

United by the solidarity of fate, Christians and non-Christians, knock at the gate of the mystery of Christ's resurrection. However, before entering, we are stopped at the threshold by the paving stone that St. Paul sends us from the dawn of time. Quoting the Old Testament, St. Paul declares: "If Christ has not been resurrected, then let's eat and drink, for tomorrow we die" (1 Corinthians 15:32; Isaiah 22:13).

I must admit that this kind of disdain for present life—even if it only refers to life on earth—shocks me profoundly. Is the atheist a mere pleasure-seeker? Even if we assume, as the atheist or non-believer would, that the resurrection is nothing but an illusion, and life is a wisp of straw, still the very fact of our frailty enables us to feel the fresh air of hope. And even if we assume that the resurrection is nothing but wind, the ephemeral nature of our humanity can make of it a clear and hopeful north wind gentle enough to allow us the fleeting joy of breathing it, if only for an exhilarating instant. There really is a human dignity in living only for today. There can be honor in living only in the present. There can be a kind of grandeur in looking nowhere but in the present for what the present may offer.

All this is true. However, according to the testimony of even non-believers, as naturally as one may feel inspired to exalt the beauty of life, it is impossible to overlook the disenchantment of all those who have ultimately been disappointed. Thus, Camus in his love of life encounters the absurd, and rebels, as all must who refuse to resign themselves to being merely "someone somewhere."

A Happy Fool

The Christian is not a happy, oblivious fool. He's certain he hasn't been "had" during his life. The resurrection proclaims the success of all life. Not only is life on earth worth living for its own sake, but the efforts we make to live good lives are also never wasted. The resurrection is no superstructure thrust upon life to give it a meaning it wouldn't have otherwise. Nor is the resurrection the glitter of a final reward that justifies, in the present, the insults of existence. The resurrection does not eliminate the tragedies in our lives. With the atheist, the Christian is confronted by the absurd. Faith isn't the negation of the absurd, it is only a way of dealing with it. And faith is just as capable of dealing with life at those times when it seems to have become sheer madness. In fact, faith itself requires a bit of madness. For the Christian doesn't touch that toward which he reaches. Like everyone else, he must face suffering, death, oblivion. A mother, next to her child's corpse, may believe in the resurrection; but this doesn't mean that the resurrection will restore her child. Such belief may give a meaning to suffering, but it doesn't remove it. Thus, the Christian resents the non-believer who says to him: "You're really lucky that you believe in the afterlife!" Yes, faith is reassuring because it has certainty in it, but this doesn't make it a security blanket. Faith is assurance in life, but it does not assure comfort. Yes, it is good to have faith. But the promise of faith is offered to everyone.

Be that as it may, it seems futile to confine oneself to these questions. What's the use of wondering whether or not it's easier to live as a Christian or non-Christian? Can't everyone choose? Believers and non-believers are alike when it comes to being human beings. That's what counts in the end. If I were told that a Christian is less of a human being because he's a Christian, I would go so far as to say I'd prefer him to be more human and less Christian. But this is an absurd argument. It's impossible for a Christian not to be more of a human being in his faith. To live as a Christian is to live in terms of Him who is fully human, the risen Christ. And ultimately, the resurrection is our chief concern because it represents the great hope and promise for mankind.

It is in the light of non-belief and belief that we must now try to understand the relation between faith and resurrection. One can't have faith without believing in the resurrection. One can't believe in the resurrection without having faith.

This seesawing invites us to examine the weight of the mystery and take stock of the assertion: "If Christ has not been resurrected, then our faith is in vain."

· Facing Facts
The Reality of History

When we speak about the resurrection, the first thing that comes to mind is the Easter experience. It includes all the strange and obscure events of those three days that shook the earth. These events constitute a fact inscribed in the annals of history. In Jerusalem, at the start of our era, when Caiaphas was high priest and Pilate governor, Jesus the Nazarene was condemned to death and then rose again on Easter morning. Although it occurred in the past, this historical fact of the death and resurrection of Christ is of the present; for beyond its historicity, it bears a spiritual reality that is the very basis of the Christian experience: The Easter mystery. In this way, the resurrection is an event of faith. An event that is an advent, for in faith, something is always happening. Something other than what I can prove. What happens is that the risen Christ communicates something of himself to me. He communicates himself to me with life-giving strength; he makes of my life something more than the facts of my daily existence. The horizons of my life are vastly expanded by what happens to me in Jesus Christ. For the believer, the resurrection constitutes a *now* whose reality transcends all that has come before.

Ultimately, the resurrection has no force unless it is recognized in faith as a present event that can change one's life. In other words, the resurrection, *experienced* at a moment of time by Jesus Christ, is an historical reality. And when it is *experienced* today by Christians who adhere to the Easter mystery, it is a truth that transcends history. Yet it is extremely important that one not detach the transcendent aspect from the historical aspect. If the resurrection of Christ had not been experienced by a person in history, one could take it for a myth, a figment of the imagination. Since Christians today experience the Easter mystery in terms of the historical fact of the resurrection, it is essential to locate the event of faith in the historical space of that initial fact. This is part of the reality of faith.

Establishing the historical fact of the resurrection is a difficult undertaking. (Everything written here is inspired by a remarkable article by Father Pousset in *Cahiers d'Action religieuse et sociale*: "Le Christ est ressuscité.") As a *fact*, the resurrection *is* historical. As an event of faith, the resurrection is a mystery eluding the investigatory methods of science. The modern historiographic technique, based on a certain sense of objectivity, is useless when dealing with facts whose interrelation and chronology do not correspond to the usual criteria of the historian. The chief difficulty lies in the unique character of the event. The resurrection story is unprecedented. No one saw Christ rise. Christ himself said nothing about how it happened. And yet no one can deny that *something* did happen. It's true that the disciples testified, but they could only give partial testimony—since they were discussing an accomplished fact. No one saw Christ pass from death to life. This act of passing from death to life does indeed elude historical verification.

The disciples were like witnesses who, after seeing a car pass them on a highway, find it a few seconds later in a ditch. Arriving at the scene of the accident, they can surmise, presume causes; they can interpret. But just what really happened? Did the driver feel faint? Did he doze off? Did he do something wrong? Did something go wrong in the car? Who can tell? One tries to reconstruct and understand. One can never know for sure exactly what took place. Nevertheless, one can establish that there *was* an accident. Making all due allowance, the same holds true, more or less, for the resurrection. No one saw Christ come back to life (and for good reason! The resurrection is not an action that can be materialized.) However, the witnesses were certain that he *had* come back to life. In an accident, one can refer back to analogous things that occurred somewhere else. But how can you do this in regard to the Resurrected? You have to bow to results.

The tomb is empty. That's important evidence. It indicates that the dead man is gone. But his disappearance is no proof of resurrection. At most, it confronts us with the fact of a change. You may say perhaps that Saint Matthew offers a concrete description: "All at once, there was a violent earthquake, for the angel of the Lord, descending from heaven, came and rolled away the stone and sat on it. His face was like lightning, his robe white as snow. The guards were so shaken, so frightened of him, that they were like dead men" (Matthew 28:2–3). This scenario, like the tale of the Ascension, comes from the same literary genre as the accounts of the manifestations of Yahweh in the Old Testament. Saint Matthew doesn't claim to recount what happened; but drawing on the traditional trappings of the Old Testament, he tries to make us understand that God manifested himself.

What about Christ's appearances? Delicate terrain on which we can't venture without understanding what the Gospels are. They are not simply reports of facts, but messages illuminated by meaningful words and facts. Thus, it comes as no surprise that the settings and the chronology of the appearances are tied to a framework meaningful to the individual Evangelist. For the events of the resurrection, Saint Luke, the evangelist of nations and universal salvation, chose, for unity of place and time, Jerusalem and the twenty-four hours of a single day. Jerusalem—the capital city of salvation. A single day—the fullness of the twenty-four-hour cycle symbolizing the universal range of the event in space and time. In Saint Matthew, a Jew addressing Jews raised on the Old Testament, the chosen setting is the mountain and the time forty days.

This literary license shouldn't make us think that the evangelists were easygoing about historical reality. Their license reflects Christ's free way of manifesting himself, now as a fisherman, now as a gardener, now as a wayfarer. Their distance from the historical reality indicates that the reality of the resurrection is totally different from human perception of reality.

The Realism of Faith

To acknowledge this historical reality, to admit its limits and, at the same time, to perceive a different system of reality inherent in faith—such is the realism of faith. Ultimately, the appearances of the risen Christ to the apostles can have reality in faith alone. These appearances can only be perceived by faith. This doesn't mean that they were figments of the disciples' imaginations or that Christ did not really show himself; it simply means that these appearances cannot be materialized. These appearances are like signs allowing Christ to make himself known, and to assign a mission to the disciples; they are not signs of evidence waiting for confirmation. The way Christ addresses Mary Magdalen or the apostles shows that trust is required for recognizing Christ. The tales of the appearances are very lean: there are few descriptive elements, no picturesque details. Only touches that presume an intimate complicity between the risen Christ and those well known to him. The language of the appearances always aims at showing that a new relationship is established between Jesus and mankind. Hence, we must carefully reread all the tales of appearances, which, obviously, are anything but anecdotes about people meeting again. At times, these appearances are disturbing. They are far more problematical than conclusive. The Gospel didn't try to camouflage anything that might be contradictory. . . . It didn't attempt to reconcile the irreconcilable, or retrieve elements that might seem more probable. This fundamental honesty, notes Father Pousset, reveals the ultimate intention of the evangelists: not to demonstrate a doctrine on the basis of facts that impose themselves on us, but to bring about faith in the same way that Christ engendered it, to make it spring from the core of a vital experience.

The primary concern of the Gospel is catechetic, not

apologetic. The evangelists were preoccupied not with proving the resurrection, but with taking into account the Mystery of Life by which Christ's disciples lived. The evangelists were not hermits isolated in a desert of inspiration, trying to revive memories of the Master. Linked with a community of believers, they expressed the faith of this community. In this way, the "authority" of the Christian communities, who witnessed the Easter event, is a determinant in authenticating the truthfulness of the faith in resurrection. Today, we still believe what those communities believed. The first Christians didn't give us proof of the resurrection; they communicated their faith in the resurrection. There is no evidence of the resurrection other than the living testimony of the first disciples and the experience of faith of the Christian communities. This is the treasure of the living Tradition that is the basis for the realism of faith. If one had to speak about proof no matter what, one would have to say that the proof of the resurrection is proof only for believers.

If God Did Not Raise Christ to Life

If God did not raise Christ to life, there is no reason to believe in God. The resurrection is an object of faith. The way in which the risen Christ appeared teaches us that we must first have faith in order to recognize him. Strictly speaking, the resurrection cannot prove the divinity of Jesus Christ, for in order to believe in his divinity, we must first believe in God. We must first admit that it was God who brought the Son back to life. Saint Paul states as much in the Letter to the Romans (6:4 and 8:11). The Acts of the Apostles repeats it in many ways (2:24; 10:40): it is the Father who, with the power of Love, has exalted the Son. It was not for the Son to justify himself, to reveal by a dazzling action that he was God; this was the job of Him who had sent him: the Father. This exaltation of the Son by the Father is nothing but the manifestation of the full possession of the Spirit dwelling in Christ. It is the glory. The Ascension reflects the glory of the resurrection. Here too, Acts insists that the resurrection is an action of the Spirit (Acts 1:2). The word *glory* should not be taken in a restrictive sense. It obviously has nothing to do with the pride of success. It is the divine condition, spoken of by Saint Paul, the very transcendence of God: Father, Son, and Spirit.

Thus, only if one believes that Jesus is the Son of God can one agree that God could bring him back to life. The resurrection is not a priori evidence of the divinity; rather, it atests to the authenticity of the mission of Jesus Christ as the envoy of the Father: if Jesus Christ is resurrected, it is because he is the Elect, the Messiah, the Son of the living God.

The purpose of salvation is summed up in the resurrected Jesus Christ—as presented by Saint Paul throughout his letters:

> In Christ, God unites all things (Ephesians 1:10).
>
> In Christ, we are one body (Romans 12:5).
>
> In Christ, we are all one (Galatians 3:28).
>
> In Christ, God reconciled the world to himself (2 Corinthians 5:19).
>
> In Christ, God's love is manifested (Romans 8:39).
>
> In Christ, we are new creations (2 Corinthians 5:17).

—2—

Jesus: Someone Who Communicates

The Resurrection II

Someone may ask, "How are dead people raised, and what sort of body do they have when they come back?" These are stupid questions. Whatever you sow in the ground has to die before it is given new life and the thing that you sow is not what is going to come; you sow a bare grain, say of wheat or something like that, and then God gives it the sort of body that he has chosen: each sort of seed gets its own sort of body.

Everything that is flesh is not the same flesh: there is human flesh, animal flesh, the flesh of birds, and the flesh of fish. Then there are heavenly bodies and there are earthly bodies; but the heavenly bodies have a beauty of their own and the earthly bodies a different one. The sun has its brightness, the moon a different brightness, the stars another brightness, and the stars differ from each other in brightness. It is the same with the resurrection of the dead: the thing that is sown is perishable but what is raised is imperishable; the thing that is sown is contemptible but what is raised is glorious; the thing that is sown is weak but what is raised is powerful; when it is sown it embodies the soul, when it is raised it embodies the spirit.

(I Corinthians 15:35–44).

• Like a Spring . . .

Like a spring that can't be prevented from welling up, the resurrection is the irresistible fountain of God's vitality. It bursts forth into human life. A nonviolent eruption. Don't picture a raging torrent, or a waterfall. Don't imagine thunder and lightning. This is a force that moves in the deepest level of our lives. A continuous flow as in a natural pool hollowed out by seeping water. The resurrection is like a river surging from the depths of man. An estuary of the most powerful source of life. Primal energy. Ultimate energy. It overcomes everything: death and sin, space and time, all accident and all necessity, all physics and all metaphysics. It is what is to come for mankind.

• Improbable but True
Faith, Credulity, and Credibility

Improbable but true, the resurrection intrigues us. It eludes science, but science does not elude it and yet the resurrection remains the focus of much study. Mystery will not be locked within the limits of human knowledge, but it nonetheless remains an object of human knowledge. That's why theology bases its reflexions on sciences with erudite names: exegesis (study of Scripture in the original Hebrew and Greek); hermeneutics (the science of interpreting the meaning of words); epistemology (the critique of the method of knowledge). As far as these efforts may go, they will never manage to take full account of the phenomenon of the resurrection. And yet, who can deny its reality? For the positivist who trusts only what science verifies, the resurrection is "unbelievable." Thus, at times, the unbeliever is tempted to think that the believer is joking with him in claiming that the basis of faith is the "unbelievable" event of the resurrection.

Hence, the resurrection asks the question of faith in terms of credibility: this means that one should not only establish the truth of the historical fact of the resurrection, but also explain the incredible fact of present-day Christian acceptance of the resurrection. There is a certain reality of the resurrection beyond a doubt. True, it would be unwarranted to take for granted the authenticity of the historical fact of the resurrection simply because Christians live in terms of that reality. But don't we have the right to wonder how far the credulity of millions of people can go; for after all, is it possible that a man can believe in the unbelievable? At the risk of being reproached for indulging in apologetics, one can ask this question: "What makes faith credible today?" It's possible, I feel, to advance along two lines:

—Faith offers a coherent vision of the world and man;
—Faith verifies this coherence in life.

Knowing How to Live

Christianity is reproached both for being simplistic and for being complex. The naïveté of the stories in the Old

Testament, the childlike tone of the parables and certain utterances in the Gospels can make Christianity seem like a religion for people with no intellectual demands. In contrast, the difficulty of certain texts, for instance the Letter to the Hebrews or the Letter to the Romans, the subtlety of theological discourses, etc., give the impression of a religion for an educated elite capable of penetrating the obscure knowledge of specialists. This double reproach paradoxically brings out the two criteria of the credibility of faith, and we can now focus on these two criteria as fruits of the resurrection. Faith is coherent. Faith is practical. It is knowing how to live. The art of faith is teaching people to relate knowledge to life.

Faith Is Practice

Not performing rites, to be sure, but the practicing of the Word of Life. Faith is action. It's already been said: there is no abstract truth in Christianity. Life is not a principle, but someone, God. And God is not an intellectual. He reveals himself not as the Thinking Being, the Purely Existing, but as someone who works ceaselessly (John 5:17). God is an activist. He's always doing something. He's creative. He spends his time loving. Loving keeps one busy. God takes his eternity to achieve the Absolute Act until infinity: Love.

When God speaks, he acts. Thus, when the risen Jesus reveals himself to Paul, he is not content to give him ideas, he manifests himself in the action of the Resurrected: He is He who changes a situation. He is He who transforms hearts. He converts. The risen Christ communicates his power to act, the energy of his Spirit to man.

The relationship of Christians to God is a relationship of action. If someone claims to love God without loving his brother, he's a liar. Love is action. Faith is the living of this active love. The Christian can't get at the mystery of the resurrection unless he commits his life to the reality that he wishes to deepen. The essence of what God asks us to believe is the essence of what he asks us to live. Many people who cannot believe cannot live. Many people don't know how to believe because they don't know how to live. But faith is not only a knowledge of life, it is knowledge in all meanings of the term.

Faith Is Coherent

Faith is "praxis," that is, knowledge put in action. There is a coherence between thinking and acting. The multiple focuses on each man, on each thing, on the world always cross the unique vision of God, who is always faithful to himself as the risen Christ. The Revelation is a corpus of doctrine in which everything holds together. But this does not make faith a closed system. Since the risen Christ is always totally different from anything one can imagine, Christian faith will never be done with questioning itself. It always seeks what God gives it to find. Nevertheless it does not seek as though there were no foundation. It has reference points which must be respected if the search is not to be transformed into a hodgepodge.

Faith is doctrine, but this doesn't make Christians doctrinaire. The doctrine of the Gospel is creative: "The letter kills, the Spirit brings to life." Faith involves dogmatic thinking, but this doesn't mean Christians have to be stuck in definitions. Faith has an inner coherence, but this doesn't make it an ideology. For centuries, Thomism may have been *the* philosophy of the Church, but today one can't say that Christianity has any particular philosophy. Philosophers, including those in the science of man and the humanities, interpret the overall meaning of the truths of faith. These truths are not detached and disconnected pieces. They form a structured whole.

Faith can be credible only to those who enter this totality. The Eiffel Tower could not stay erect on one leg. Faith will not stay erect judged by one dogma. Faith finds its coherence in the resurrection. The resurrection is the keystone of the edifice. If it weren't held up by the thrust of all the other stones, it would crash to earth. If one reflects on the resurrection detached from the whole of the Christian mystery, one is doomed not only not to understand it, but not to understand anything else.

If one wishes to live in the harmony of what God gives us to know, one cannot disregard the intelligence of faith. To look at its structure, to understand the Spirit of its laws— this is the goal of reflecting on the resurrection.

• The Law of Couples
Permanence. Newness

Christ resurrected is communicative. He transmits the essential of himself to man: the power of his resurrection. Christ passes the reality of his life through man's desire to live. He makes people want to live more and more intensely. Live today more than yesterday, and live tomorrow today. Live today the Today of the World. Live on. Live forever. We are passionately interested in the resurrection, because it is a hint of the life beyond the one we are living, beyond what we know. Christ's resurrection, the prototype of our resurrection, offers us a glimpse of what will happen one fine morning—the morning of our Easter—when we will see Christ face to face and he will sing to us: "Charles, Bill, Mary, Jean, wake up, you who are asleep, arise from the dead!" Radically transformed by this unforeseeable passage from death to life, we will be perfectly ourselves and totally different. We will discover ourselves to be wonderfully identical with what we may have known as the best of ourselves and amazingly changed. At last, we will find ourselves again while finding ourselves altogether different. At last, we will know ourselves and recognize others. At last, "we will know as we are known." We will be able to say to someone else: "Tell me." That is, reveal me to myself! At last—oh beautiful "at last"—every end will be new!

No one has ever come back from the dead. Manifestly, Jesus alone returned. But he said just about nothing—or almost nothing. He sketched the image of what is to come. He asks every man from now on to draw those characteristics which are his in his fondest dreams. As though in the blurred reflections of ancient mirrors, he lets us catch a glimpse of what we need in order to live in hope. We must respect this lack of certainty. We must love the fact that thanks to God, man always has life to discover. Let's not try to imagine how things are going to come about. We run the risk of going astray. Considering the strange things we still hear today from Christian lips, it may not be pointless to repeat the obvious.

The resurrection of bodies is not going to be some kind of

better reincarnation. The resurrection is obviously not a re-incarnation in a different body. By coming back to life himself, Christ shows us that a person can be truly and fully himself only in the essential unity of body and soul. This unity is not a restructuring after death according to a re-vised and corrected version of the old physical model. At death, the body is still something of what it was. It then decomposes and finally disappears. Now, it's nothing. On a metaphysical level, however, the meaning of this body still exists: the person's body remains substantially what it has always been—a principle of communication and an expres-sion of relationship. By means of the resurrection, the body is reintegrated in a new way in its essential function of re-lationship. We now become capable of understanding and being understood, of being reattached to people without being tied to them. It thus has a different mode of relating: it is, as Saint Paul terms it, incorruptible. It finds a different mode of presence, that of the Spirit. Christ communicates the power of his Spirit to us. The Father's action in resur-recting the Son in the strength of the Spirit is thus endlessly actualized in every resurrected human being.

Man is reborn in the Spirit to the new life of God. This is what Ezekiel announced: "I shall put my spirit in you and you will live. . . . Come from the four winds, Spirit, breathe on these dead; let them live" (Ezekiel 37:14,9). This second birth according to the Spirit is manifested in the sacramen-tal order by baptism. Christ told Nicodemus: No one can en ter the Kingdom if he is not reborn (John 3:1–16). When he is resurrected, man is henceforth known as "reborn." He is the New Human Being, a new creature, according to the model of Christ.

Paul affirms that Christ's "unspiritual body" (Romans 7:14) becomes a "spiritual body" (I Corinthians 15:44) through the resurrection. An unspiritual body? A spiritual body? How can we align these apparently so contradictory terms? What body is meant? What spirituality? *Spiritual* is too often used as the opposite of *physical*, as though the physical were nothing but the material, as though matter were entirely subject to mind. Too often we draw a dichotomy between what are conventionally known as matter and mind, body and soul. In this respect, Plato, Aristotle, and Descartes weigh heavily on Christian thought. When we recall that for centuries the body was considered the prison of the soul, it comes as no surprise that Christians could picture the resurrection as a reanimation of a corpse. The resurrection is not the power of the soul to recover a bodily envelope. Biblical tradition forbids our assuming such a dualism between body and soul, matter and mind. As a being of flesh, man is a person, both in body and spirit. Christ's resurrection is the sign of this fundamental unity.

In the expression "spiritual body," *spiritual* refers to the Spirit of God and not to the human mind. The Spirit of God is not simply an abstract intellectual principle, it is the person of God offering himself. To believe is to enter into a relationship with God. In this sense faith is a mode of spiritual relationship. Can't you see that, in God, the Spirit is Himself this "spiritual body," the archetype of any spiritual body?

The Spirit establishes an absolute freedom. The passage from death to life brings out this sovereign freedom, which Christ possesses fully. Christ can appear to his disciples anywhere. He is not limited by space or time. He communicates as he likes, thereby revealing to us that his glorious body declares the Spirit's presence.

This language may seem abstruse to some people. What else can we say but Paul's words to the community in Corinth: "The depths of a man can only be known by his own spirit." In other words, one must already have an aptitude for inner life in order to penetrate the language taught by the Spirit, expressing realities of the spirit in terms of the spirit (I Corinthians 2:11, 13).

Identity. Difference

When we are resurrected, we will be the same and altogether different. It is of cardinal importance to understand this balancing of permanence and newness; for we cannot deal with the Christian mystery without referring to this specific dynamism of the resurrection. Thus, as we shall see, one cannot achieve understanding of the Sacrament Church unless one enters into the dialogue of identity and difference, that is, the unity in which I find myself both self-identical and a new creature.

What does this mean? The resurrected human being is not a different person, but a person who is altogether different. The change of condition doesn't alter the person's identity: it recreates it. In the unity of his being, the resurrected person is his own alter ego. The paradoxical ways in which Jesus appears to Thomas and Mary Magdalen emphasize the continuity and rupture so often found in the behavior of the risen Christ. To Thomas, Jesus wants to stress that, although resurrected, he is still himself. Still the same, he says: "Hold out your hand and put it into my side"

(John 20:24–28). To Mary Magdalen, however, Jesus wishes to point out the other aspect: he is himself, but altogether different. So he says equivalently: "Do not touch me, do not hold me back" (John 20:11–18). But to make her understand that nevertheless it really is himself, Jesus addresses her by name: "Mary!" He likewise says to the apostles: "It is I!"

Some people may think that the risen Christ is not a very communicative Christ. A pronoun! Yes. "It is I." That's how the Lord refers to himself. Existentially, that's how Claudel expresses himself in *Break of Noon*: "Mesa, I am Ysé, it is I." "Peter, Jack, Bill, Harriet, I am Jesus." He prefers to present himself subjectively: "It is I." If the name refers to the person, the pronoun *I* more effectively indicates the possession of the subject. It's the person taking charge of himself. He designates himself in his relationship to the other. The resurrection introduces us into this world of relationship, where the person can say, "I am the same yet altogether different." This relationship is that of faith. To live in faith is to make the relationship between life, man, and God.

· Thinking Clearly . . .

Because Jesus Christ is resurrected, living one's life means fulfilling the words of the creed, "I believe in God," with all the love of the life that Jesus presented to us. It means proclaiming: "I believe in man."

Because Jesus is risen, living one's life means fulfilling the words of Genesis, "be fruitful and multiply," with all the hope of Christ's prayer: "Your kingdom come!" It means proclaiming:

"I believe in Him who is to come
I believe in that which is to come."

We must distinguish between the *future* and *that which is to come*. To believe in the future is to believe in man, to hope that humanity will some day become more human. It means believing in the world and doing everything to make sure the world achieves its end. But if we believe Simone de Beauvoir, it also means choosing to believe that man has an end and that the end of the world is truly an end, a hole, a void.

If we listen to the most recent songs of the disenchanted French pop singer Léo Ferré, who cries at the top of his lungs "No God and no master," one can't help panicking at the nothingness of a world that makes Ferré bellow out: "to die for nothing and to live for everything." He needs all his wind power, the shattering range of the mike, and the frenzy of the Olympia concert hall on a Saturday night, to foretell, or rather foreshout, a derisory future that we ultimately dare not believe in. "In ten thousand years, we'll be everything," he sings. Ten thousand years. Ten thousand centuries. This is not the time to come, it is merely a fragment of time. . . .

Belief in the future is the faith of the unbeliever. However, belief in what is to come is belief in the New Human Being, is hope that man will some day be different. It is belief in the world and a willingness to do anything so that the Kingdom may some day come. It is belief that something will always happen, because the Kingdom will not end. Belief in what is to come is belief in Him who was and who is coming. Belief in the time to come is the faith of the

Christian! "Your kingdom come!" Let what is to come come!

The heaven sought by the Christian is not a golden palace for disillusioned rich people. The New World of the Resurrection is a perpetual becoming in which we will discover:

> Man greater and greater
> God more and more overwhelming
> Happiness happier and happier
> Beauty more and more beautiful
> Life livelier and livelier
> Light brighter. . . .
> Like the glowing clarity of the infinite spaces
> of contemplation.

3

Jesus: Someone Who Makes a Sign

The Sacrament Church

This mystery that has now been revealed through the Spirit to his holy apostles and prophets was unknown to any men in past generations; it means that pagans now share the same inheritance, that they are parts of the same body, and that the same promise has been made to them, in Christ Jesus, through the Gospel. I have been made the servant of that Gospel by a gift of grace from God who gave it to me by his own power. I, who am less than the least of all the saints, have been entrusted with this special grace, not only of proclaiming to the pagans the infinite treasures of Christ but also of explaining how the mystery is to be dispensed. Through all the ages, this has been kept hidden in God, the creator of everything. Why? So that the Sovereignties and Powers should learn only now, through the Church, how comprehensive God's wisdom really is, exactly according to the plan which he had from all eternity

in Christ Jesus our Lord. This is why we are bold
enough to approach God in complete confidence,
through our faith in him (Ephesians 3:5–12).

• "Christ Loved the Church"

"Christ loved the Church." Are we touched by this
utterly simple revelation? Like seashells, the purest words,
the clearest phrases, are eventually drained of their substance.

"Christ loved the Church." What was there in God's
heart that made Christ, through all ages, love the Church?

Christ still loves the Church. What is there in the hearts
of the baptized that makes so many Christians appear to ne-
glect, mistreat their own body, the Church, the Body of
Christ?

Christ gave himself for the Church. How could Christ's
passion for the Church leave us indifferent? Faith can only
be loving. I mean that one can't approach the mystery of
the Church merely by asking intellectual questions.

Christ loved the Church. Do we even *like* the fact that
Christ loves the Church?

• The Church, a Revealing Screen
*The Sacraments of the Church and the Sacrament
Church*

Several times the Council of Vatican II used the
word *sacrament* to describe the Church. But I note that
Christians did not wait for these theologians to experience
the richness of the Sacrament Church.

The Sacrament Church: what are we talking about? It is not so much a matter of seeking a definition as a certain way of understanding how the Sacrament Church assumes its calling to unite the World. The point is not to redefine the Church, but to see it in its relationship to the world—and this in the light of what we know about the way of Jesus' presence since his resurrection.

The Sacrament Church is the title of a report that Monsignor Coffy presented to the assembly of French bishops at Lourdes in November 1971. It was published under the title of *The Church, A Sign of Salvation in the Midst of Men*. This describes as compactly as possible the substance of the three words: the Sacrament Church.

We are more used to hearing about the sacraments *of* the Church than the Sacrament Church. These two roll over each other the way ocean billows break into foam on the shore, becoming a single wave. Their reality is really one and the same. A fruitful interaction occurs. The sacraments make the Church and the Church makes the sacraments. The Church draws upon the power of the Spirit of the risen Christ in setting up the signs that Jesus established as sacraments. The Church is nourished by the very signs that it helps bring to birth and that help give birth to the Church. The Church grows by means of the sacraments, but at the same time it is always greater than they. The Sacrament Church is not enclosed in the domain of the seven sacraments. In celebrating the sacraments, the Church manifests that which is at its inmost core: the sign of Christ, the sacrament of Christ. The sacraments merely express this fruitfulness. In everything it is, in everything it does, the Church signifies Christ. The Church is called a sacrament because it received from Christ the power of setting up the signs of his sacramental presence. Thus, it was not, for instance, Jesus on earth who directly instituted the sacrament of unction for the sick, but the Spirit of the risen Jesus inspiring the disciples of the first Christian community.

The Vision of Faith

A sacrament is the visible sign of an invisible reality. For instance, the bread and wine of the Eucharist are the sign of the real and hidden presence of Jesus' death and resurrection. To state that the Church is a sacrament is to affirm that, by its public life, the Church manifests the salvation of Jesus Christ in the midst of human beings. This is a fine assertion, but how theoretical! The Church, far from being acknowledged by the world as the sign of salvation, is often viewed as an insurmountable obstacle in the quest for God. Claiming to be a sign, it is certainly an improbable paradox for the Church to be considered a screen. A paradox that has the advantage of bringing out the nature of the sign in question, for it is a sign discernable only to the eyes of faith.

Sit down in front of your TV set. Before switching it on, you can't see anything or hear anything. And the Church, so long as it's not switched on by faith, remains an opaque screen for the world. The signs of salvation it emits can be received only if they are seen with the eyes of faith: farsighted and beyond the reproaches that can be made against the Church.

Needing to have the eyes of faith in order to discern the sign does not mean that the opacity caused by sin in the Church is illusory and unimportant. Many people of good

will would be willing to believe, but cannot, precisely because of the smoke screen caused by sin. These remarks are
meant simply to underscore the necessity of a radical conversion, not only in nonbelievers, but also in the Church,
which, because of the interference of its sinning, makes itself inaudible and provokes nonbelief.

It would be pointless to wipe away the dust that dims the
clarity of a TV screen if you didn't first make sure that the
set was working. And similarly, it would be pointless to ar-
range the Church in such a way as to make it credible, reli-
able, if one didn't care about faith being born in human
hearts. If we are to give and receive faith, we have to pay
attention to the means of transmission. There can be no
Christian faith without the believer's agreement to meet
God through the mediation of the signs he asks of us. In this
sense, the Sacrament Church is the revealing screen that
allows us to discover the hidden reality of God's design
through the Word and the sacraments which the Church
has been transmitting since the days of the apostles.

• The Christian Faith Depends
on the Sacrament Church
The Form of Faith Is Sacramental

The Resurrection is the center of our faith, not only
because it points to the essence of our faith, but also because
it seals forever and always God's relationship with man in
the heart of the Christian faith. Jesus Christ resurrected is
spiritually present in the world and the source of God's relationship with man. This relationship belongs to the order of
signs. Let's say it again: When one speaks of the spirituality
of the risen Christ, one means that since the resurrection,

Jesus has been in full possession of the person of the Spirit. In consequence he has the power to make himself present in a universal manner. There is obviously a gap between Jesus Christ's presence outside time and space and the conditions of human existence, which is limited by time and space. For communicating between the extraterrestrial and the terrestrial, there is no other tongue common to both God and man than the language of signs, the sacramental language.

The Sacrament Church is the place par excellence of this language, for, as a sign of Jesus Christ, it makes Christ's mediation between God and man possible. By the same token, the Church can also tell us how faith functions.

When I say *functions*, I realize I'm using a term that could make it seem as if faith comes by techniques. There are no techniques of faith, only a coherence, a specificity. The act of believing corresponds in man to a certain way of perceiving spiritual things, and in God to a design for salvation, which he reveals to us through the great totality of sacraments that is the Sacrament Church. In other words, the act of believing presupposes a certain design in both God and man . . . . We must know how faith works, for if faith doesn't work, then it is in vain.

By the light of the Sacrament Church, we are able to respond to the well-known question of the incompatibility of faith with the scientific, technological mentality—in short, with the modern world. In an age so influenced by rationalism and efficiency, the future of the Christian faith lies with the Sacrament Church.

Faith has a sacramental design. This pronouncement is as terse and rigorous as a theorem but can be put in more familiar terms: *You don't meet God face to face.*

The act of believing presupposes a system of references, an order of things. The scientist conducting an experiment doesn't do just any sort of research in just any sort of way; he guides his experiment according to recognized laws. And similarly, the believer doesn't look for God in a helter-skelter way. He relies on a given system. Hence, we can state that even if the content of the faith of the beatitudes were utterly insane and utopian, yet the act of believing in it is based on a reasonable system. It is with full knowledge of the facts that one accepts something which is not exclusively scientific.

We Do Not Meet God Face to Face
The Experience of Damascus

When Jesus was on earth, the apostles and everyone else who approached him met him face to face. That's obvious. After the resurrection, the stories about his appearances indicate that the disciples again met him face to face. He told Saint Thomas: "Put your fingers on my side." (John 20:24-28). According to one interpretation, Thomas had tangible contact with Jesus. But we know that this contact was ambiguous, because Jesus said the opposite to Mary Magdalen: "Don't touch me." However this may be, we can presumably say that after the resurrection, those who didn't know Christ on earth met him only through his sacramental presence.

Yes. Even in the most exceptional circumstances, one meets God only by way of sacramental mediation. Thus, Saint Paul, on the road to Damascus, found God through the ministry of the Word as practiced by Ananias and through the baptism he received as authentification and as the seal of conversion.

To say that we don't meet God directly does not mean that we don't meet him personally. Christ in person addresses Paul: "Saul, Saul, why do you persecute me?" (Acts 9:4). God knows that Christ's ambush will remain the event that will explain Paul's entire life. Paul will stay marked until his final day by Christ's words "which must not and cannot be put into human language" (2 Corinthians 12:4). And even though he cannot fathom this rapture, one does not question the reality of his vision. But this vision remains a vision of faith and not a face-to-face confrontation. Indeed, Saint Luke notes in the Acts of the Apostles: "His eyes were open, but he saw nothing." And Saint Paul himself says: "Was it in my body, was it without my body, I don't know" (2 Corinthians 12:2).

The realism of encounter granted to Paul may not be proven by scientific means, but is part of the realism of the Spirit, who establishes an intangible means of relating. To be sure, as people quickly point out, Paul's was a mystical experience—implying that mystical experience eludes the confines of sacramental mediation. Why not believe that Paul had an unprecedented "revelation," since he says so himself (2 Corinthians 12:4). But this doesn't mean that such ecstacy whisked Paul into a world different from the world of sacramental faith. If Jesus' relationship to Paul had been face to face, Christ himself would not have gone through Ananias to have Paul baptized. Indeed, we all too frequently forget this astounding and revealing fact. Paul was not exempted from baptism: the baptism crowning the episode on the road to Damascus brings the full dimension to the encounter. Paul was not baptized as a mere formality, so that he could be like the others. Rather, we should recognize baptism as a sign of an authentically sacramental faith beyond which there is no encounter with God, for it will always remain true that "no one has ever seen God."

Thus, the Word and the sacrament appear as the turning points of this mediation, in which man's encounter with God comes to full fruition. I say "full fruition" because, fortunately, many people meet God in their own way without being baptized, that is, outside the visible mediation—I was about to say the "good offices"—of the Sacrament Church. But this is no reason to discount the sacramental order. A sympathetic attitude towards the man of good will who seeks God is a positive thing. But regrettably, under the guise of generosity and tolerance, we find an accommodating laxness that discredits the sacraments, and ultimately warps God's design for salvation.

A number of biblical episodes tell of encounters between God and man through the Sacraments, for instance the tale of the Queen of Ethiopia's steward, whom Philip, the deacon, baptizes. But perhaps the most typical depiction of this is the story of the disciples going to Emmaus (Act 8: 26–39).

The Emmaus Experience

The road to Emmaus is the direction of all Christian life. All Christians in their own way are asked to relive the heart of this story, which is the story of every single one of us. Each of us in our own way, for obviously no one can imitate it exactly. We now have a detached attitude that the disciples lacked. We know things that they didn't know. Our itinerary as believers doesn't have to be a carbon copy of theirs. The point is to discern in their experience that which gives us light today. We have already meditated upon this page of the Gospel in the light of the spirituality of faith. We must now approach it from a different angle and, in the road of faith that Christ reveals to us, find the route leading to the Sacrament Church.

Let us schematically distinguish four stages which are crucial for understanding the structure of faith. These four stages form a map to help us understand the Sacrament Church.

1. A difficult approach. Christ arrives on the road incognito. He approaches the disciples and yet stays remote. His presence is so indecisive that the companions don't know with whom they're dealing.

2. A light-giving word. When Christ, in the light of the Scriptures, replays the events that have just occurred, their eyes are opened. They realize that what concerns Christ concerns them too.

3. The breaking of bread. While the disciples are aware of being in the presence of someone who is very much alive, it is only when Jesus repeats the sacramental gesture of the breaking of bread that they recognize him. It is startling to realize that Jesus was there for them, in person but unrecognized, and not until the Eucharistic action did they know him.

4. The mission of the Church. The disciples then go and tell others what they have experienced and so the Church is born and grows. To grow is its mission.

The Sacraments, Frames of Reference for Faith

Let's discuss two points: the sacraments as signs of life; and the sacraments as signs of the vitality of faith.

The Sacraments as Signs of Life

The disciples of Emmaus recognized Christ—that strange man who was both near and far—by the sacramental gesture of the interpreted Word and the breaking of bread; this gesture touched their own lives. The breaking of bread brings them into the vital experience they could have with Christ. If the disciples of Emmaus hadn't previously committed their entire lives to Christ, then this celebration of the Word and the Eucharist would never have spoken to them. The sacraments can speak only to people capable of looking at Christ's gestures and actions and recognizing in them the meaning of what they experience. The person who doesn't live in terms of Christ is not open to the sacraments. The sacraments show that the bond between faith and life is the risen Christ, who gives the power of his resurrection to the things of our every-day lives. By prolonging the incarnation of Him who was fully God and fully man, the sacraments reveal the unity of life to us: a single life that takes the entire Christian.

Obviously, if Christ says nothing, if life says nothing, then the sacraments can say nothing. The Christian who deserts life cannot understand what the sacraments mean; for the sacraments gain their meaning from what life expresses and from what God reveals of his life through the things brought to us by our lives as human beings.

Thus, not only is there no separation between the sacraments and life, but they are so close that one can state paradoxically that Christ instituted the sacraments so that Christians could avoid seeking God outside the events of their daily lives.

In this context, it is unfortunate that certain fierce militants, with a politically, a socially committed faith, can lightly say that the sacraments are pious derivatives of life for Christians who have nothing better to do. Have they noticed that the sacraments, by constantly referring to everyday life, prevent Christians from fleeing into a faith that would spell escape from that everyday life, escape from reality? But beware: the reality of life is not always as we picture it, that is, reduced to the immediate contingencies of life. The reality of life for the housekeeper is something different from the horizon of her pots and pans, her vacuuming, her shopping, her taking the kids to school. The reality of life for the businessman is something different from his wheelings and dealings, his skills and interests. The reality of life for the bureaucrat is something different from his files and reports, his administrative efforts and his weekends in the country. The reality of life for the politician is something different from his schemes, his platforms, his ambitions. Life is always bigger, always finer than our personal circumstances.

Because the sacraments are signs of life in abundance, they teach us about the greatness of our lives as children of God. They show us that the reality of life goes far beyond our ordinary daily existence. People are tempted to shrink God down to the supposedly scientific limits of reality. In order to armor Christians against this temptation, Christ established the sacraments as signs of the intrusion of his transcendence into the heart of the most ordinary human realities. I've often noticed that the people who pride themselves most on being realists will boil realism down to a certain way of living in accordance with the spirit of the world, a certain business sense, a certain knowledge of human motives, a certain skill in coping with the law of the jungle—in short, a wise materialism that is closed off to transcendance, to the order of the Spirit, in which hidden values are as real as all the harsh beliefs that make the law of the world.

Thus, ultimately, it was to keep us from seeking God's will solely in terms of the limited reality of life, in the signs of the time, the events of the world, and the unrolling of history, that Christ instituted his sacraments as the channel of his always unexpected intervention in the midst of our human struggles.

The Sacraments, Signs of the Vitality of Faith

The Emmaus disciples teach us to recognize the risen Christ as he presents himself in our lives today. Always on the road, he never lets himself be stopped. He is a companion who is both far and near. He appears in order to disappear. He is present in absence. This alternating closeness and distance, presence and absence is the dynamic of faith that the sacraments offer through the Spirit, who forbids man to appropriate God. Indeed, because Jesus Christ gives himself to us spiritually, man can never identify with God. In the very intimacy he may have with his Lord, man always senses him as being distant. For instance, in the Eucharist, however fervent the Christian, the man who communes with God has no tangible hold on God: he doesn't touch him, doesn't see him, doesn't grasp him. The contact is beyond the tangible world. Many Christians imagine they are losing faith, because they don't have a tangible impression of a "gentle presence." If they had a better sense of the sacraments, they wouldn't be surprised at this normal state of affairs: the sacraments act as frames of reference for faith. They allow us to verify its vitality. They authenticate it by letting us measure the distance that prevents us from reducing God to our limits. Likewise, a good number of Christians feel a deep malaise towards the Church because they do not take into account the interplay of nearness and farness as manifested by the Sacrament Church: *it gathers all the parts of Christ in a single body, and it marks the distance between the gathered body and the body of the risen Christ.*

The Sacrament Church is not defined. It reveals the way of approaching God. By its very being, it teaches us what faith is.

• The Beloved Church of Jesus Christ . . .

The sacraments understood in the light of Emmaus illustrate the Christian life: Christian life is always a recognition of the risen Christ on the road. This recognition is gradual. It presumes an endlessly renewed quest that slowly leads man to discover the effectiveness of the Spirit within him: through each sacrament, the action of God bringing his Son back to life is actualized for every person. If the Church has any sign to give the world, or, more precisely, if the Church must be a sign, then it is a sign of the operative presence of the Spirit of the Resurrection in the world. The Sacrament Church is the announcement, to the world, of the Resurrection, which shapes all creation.

It's fine to speak about the Church in this way, but one can't speak about the Church without the words being prayer. Praying through and for the Church that Jesus loves:

Beloved Church of Jesus Christ . . .
Loved before we were born
Loved since the Beginning
You go with the Word
And come from the Spirit
You destine us for the Father
And gather us as brothers.

Human Church Worldly Church Real Church
When will you be without human imperfection?

Oh beloved universal Church
Your beauty surpasses human thought
Because you're always and simultaneously
The Source of Holiness in the depth of our sins
The Source of Unity in the heart of our stray impulses
The Source of Catholicity in the midst of our disparities
The Foundation, the Source of apostles
and men are such poor things
I believe in the Church that God loves.
Oh beloved Church of human beings
Beloved Church of Jesus Christ!

— 4

Jesus: Someone Who Creates
The World and the Church

He is the image of the unseen God
and the first-born of all creation,
for in him were created
all things in heaven and on earth:
everything visible and everything invisible,
Thrones, Dominations, Sovereignties, Powers—
all things were created through him and for him.
Before anything was created, he existed,
and he holds all things in unity.
Now the Church is his body,
he is its head.

As he is the Beginning
he was first to be born from the dead,
so that he should be first in every way;
because God wanted all perfection
to be found in him
and all things to be reconciled through him and
for him,

everything in heaven and everything on earth,
when he made peace
by his death on the cross. (Colossians 1:15–20)

· A Functional Architecture

"I will build my Church," said Christ. When utter-
ing these words, Jesus must have been thinking of that verse
in Wisdom, which he offers to us as a parable: "The man
who wants to build a tower starts by sitting down!" Before
putting up a construction site, you have to study the terrain, draw up blueprints, but, above all, know what you're
after.

The Church's only function is to be a sign of Christ. It
was in this spirit that Jesus pictured the architecture of his
Church: essentially functional. He therefore planned his
edifice as having a sacramental structure. In a word: He instituted the SACRAMENT Church.

There is no opposition between the Sacrament Church
and the Institutional Church. These two dimensions, each
in its way, overlap with the two faces of the mystery of the
invisible and the visible Church. Wishing the Church to be
the visible sign of salvation for the world, Christ gave it the
power to do so by making it sacramental. The Sacrament
Church was assigned the mission of challenging the Institutional Church about the way it actualized the signs of salvation. And the Institutional Church was assigned the mission
of challenging the Sacrament Church on the way it manifests salvation. It thus appears that the institution of the
Church is sacramental and the sacramental nature of the
Church, institutional. The Church experiences this sacra-

mental nature through its numerous institutions, which ought to put into action the announcement of salvation. Yet we know very well that institutions barely avoid suffocating life. This is why people attack the institutions of the Church (not to be confused with the Church as an institution). Here is not the place to start a debate on these institutions. Instead, let's examine a few delicate points that strike at the heart of our faith and that all have some bearing on the Sacrament Church.

Unless we always keep in mind why the Sacrament Church exists (to manifest the power of the risen Christ) one cannot possibly speak clearly about the Church.

—We all know that famous statement of Joan of Arc: "Christ and the Church are one." Can we thus identify the Church with Christ?

—Since Saint Paul, people have endlessly kept repeating: "The Church is the body of Christ." What body is meant?

—Since Vatican II, we do not dare repeat something that seemed normal at the time of the Council of Trent: "There is no salvation outside the Church." How does this statement sound today?

· **Christ and the Church: They Are Two**
   1. Similar and Different

In his report on the Sacrament Church, Monsignor R. Coffy denounces statements—no matter how celebrated —that tend to identify Christ and the Church. Thus, Bossuet tersely said: "The Church is Christ continued and spread across time and space." This underscores the continuity of the power of the Resurrection, which, on the one hand, animates the person of Christ and, on the other hand, transfigures our own persons today. Furthermore, it emphasizes the intimate communion between Christ and Christians—an intimacy so deep that Christ himself could say on the road to Damascus: "Saul, Saul, why do you persecute *Me*?" This persecution of Christians is felt by Christ as a personal attack on him. Which does not mean to say that he identifies totally with Christians.

On several occasions, we've pointed out the "sacramental law" that could be called the *law of Emmaus*: Presence in absence—distance in communion. Between Jesus and the Church, there is a certain identity, that is, a certain similarity, which comes from the power of the Resurrection communicated by the same Spirit. But there is also a concrete difference: Christ's person is not to be confused with the persons who are members of the Church. This identity/difference, similarity/difference is shown by Christ himself, as for instance, when he speaks to the disciples about his Father. He doesn't say, "Our Father," but *"My* Father" and *"your* Father." He thus indicated that he alone, the Only Begotten Son, may say: "My Father." Christians can address God as "Our Father," but not in the same way as Jesus.

This autonomy of persons achieving the purest and deepest of unions together is something that all married couples can experience. "Being one in one single flesh" (Ephesians 5:31) has never meant that two people were reduced to one. Each remains him- or herself, and yet each becomes more than him- or herself, because a new being is created, so new that we may say: "They are no longer two, they are one." However, two does not equal one. In other words, we can speak of this unity in marriage only if we also speak of identity and difference. Likewise, in the Church, one can speak of this togetherness of the community of love between Christ and Christians only if one never forgets the real independence between Christ and the Christians who live in him. The Sacrament Church is ultimately this proclamation of God's extraordinary liberty when he totally commits himself to living with human beings.

This commitment is the mystery of the Union that the Bible presents in nuptial terms. Saint Paul himself, trying to express this play of identity and difference, finds no better image for the Church than the "Bride of Christ."

This is not just a pious image. It may sound quite old-fashioned. But it's really quite up to date. It reveals in its own way that the Church is both similar to and different from Christ. Similar, because it truly participates in the life of Christ; and different, because it is not the same.

Joan of Arc, in the marvelous simplicity of her heart, perfectly understood what she told her judges: "Christ and the Church, it seems to me that they're One and the Same." Facing death at the stake, she didn't have time for theological niceties and subtle distinctions. Today, in order to be understood by a world that reproaches the Church for annexing God, we have to specify that Christ and the Church are two. This theological distinction is, beyond any doubt, one of the most valuable reflections on the Sacrament Church: the Church is not Christ, it is the sign of Christ.

This statement has an immediate *pastoral* consequence: how many people who reject the Church accuse it of taking the place of God! How many people fail to understand that the Church can call itself "Christ" and at the same time wear a robe that is not without stains or free of sin . . . ! The instant one points out this distance between Christ and the Church, it becomes plain that the Church may not be measured against itself. Its reference is Christ. One can then more readily admit that the Church is the source of holiness in the dependence on its Lord and full of sinners to the extent that it receives all human miseries in the name of the Savior.

2. *United and Distinct*

The Church is not Christ. It is of Christ. Like the father or mother who says about his or her child: "He's mine, of me." Or better: like the parents who say about their child: "He's ours, of us." Similarly, Christ could say: "The Church is mine, of me"; or rather: "According to the will of the Father and in the action of the Spirit, the Church is of us."

For parents, the child—flesh of their flesh, blood of their blood—is *their* love. For God, Father/Son/Spirit, the Church is *their* love. There is such a powerful bond between the mother and the child she carries, the child she nurses, such a powerful resemblance, that probably, when looking at her baby, she could say: "This is my body." Only probably. For the mother knows quite well that this body doesn't belong to her. This body, no matter how strong the resemblance, is her child's body. Not hers.

God, who carries all men, his children, has such a powerful bond with them, shares so deeply with them, that at the limit of his unlimited love, Christ could say about the bread that gathered all men: "This is my body." But, on Holy

Thursday, he knew quite well that his body, close to death and near to resurrection, belonged only to God. Christ's spiritual body cannot be likened to the body we form in the Church. It is the same body, for it is animated by the same Spirit, yet it is different, for the Spirit of the Resurrection gives life to the Church in a different way: the one we spoke about in regard to Paul on the road to Damascus and the disciples on the road to Emmaus. This way is sacramental. Which means that the Church is the *mediation* of this Spirit and not the literal incarnation of the body of Christ.

Since we've established that in faith one doesn't encounter God face to face, how could the Church claim to be the body of Christ visibly? It is the body of Christ only sacramentally, that is the real presence of Jesus Christ resurrected, through the sign that the Church constitutes. To be this sign is nothing. One shouldn't think we discredit the Church by stating that it is only the sacramental body of Christ, a sign of this body. In fact, the Church has the unheard-of power to establish a communion of life between all the members who profess faith in the same God, recognizing themselves and one another as united in the same Lord. The Church incorporates us in Christ by forming a bond with him, and yet it marks the distance between the resurrected Christ and ourselves. The Church unites but points to the difference.

This perpetual seesawing of communion and distance was something that Paul felt keenly when proposing the image of Christ as the head of the Church. "Christ is the head of the Church, which is his body" (Ephesians 1:22). This image locates Christ's original place in the body we form with him. It marks the distinction that must always be made between the personal body of the resurrected Christ and the Churchly body that we form with him. By saying "the Church . . . is his body," Saint Paul is by no means claiming that Christ is lost in the crowd. He is pointing out the very opposite, namely that Christ forms the Church. Christ too felt the need for such a distinction; in his allegory of the Vine, he doesn't believe it unnecessary to explain: "You are the shoots and I am the Vinestock" (John 15:1). Christ is the whole of the vine, but he is also the stock, which shouldn't be confused with the shoots.

This focus on the Church body in the light of the Sacrament Church has a vast pastoral consequence. Too often, the lack of precise thinking about the Church, the body of Christ, would make it seem that the Church encloses all of God's vitality within itself, as though the Spirit were paralyzed except through the members of the Church. This focus also has an eschatological consequence, that is, a significance for our total destiny, for the end of time.

To say that the Church is the sacrament of Christ's body is to attempt to explain that the Church carries within itself an invisible reality that surpasses it while it grows without ceasing: the Kingdom of God. The Church is not the Kingdom of God, but only the hope thereof. The hope for the New World, which is to come and is already here. All human beings are ultimately invited to the Kingdom. The Church is here, bearing this invitation, announcing to the world that the Kingdom is already here, because Jesus is risen, and yet still is to come since we are asked to make his resurrection ours. "Because the Church is the Sacrament of the Kingdom," says Monsignor Coffy, "its first mission is to exist as a sign of this kingdom."

Thus, the Church cannot orbit around itself; it is not its own center. It cannot stop with itself; it is not its own end. It is only to the extent of being destined to become the total Christ—recapitulating all creation—that the Church is an end for itself. But this end transcends it, for Christ will always be greater than the Church. Because God is not confined to the Church, one cannot claim, strictly speaking, that the People of God is reduced to the Church. The Church is the direction in which these people are heading, the developing growth of these people, that is, the place where we hear, where we see, where we celebrate the transformation of the world into a New World.

3. *Useless but Indispensable*

While some people tend to view the Church, Christ's Body, as an end in itself, others reduce it to being a mere means for going to God, an unavoidable intermediary.... This is a materializing conception of the Church, and also a minimizing one, for ultimately, one can always find another means and one can always do without an intermediary. The Church is not just an instrument.

The Church is the place of Christ's passage into the world. I would therefore say that the Church is the normal way, but not an obligatory one. When you're in the mountains and trying to climb a peak, you find trails marked out, perhaps lined with survey poles, indicating the safest route. This doesn't mean that other roads are prohibited, or that you won't reach your goal if you take any other path than the one indicated. You're simply showing that you're outside the norms....

God doesn't oblige people to pass through the Church by threatening them, by setting up regulations, by issuing vetoes. He reveals that the gift of his love passes through the channels of salvation that he has foreseen according to his benevolent design since ages ago . . . . Hence, to declare that "there is no salvation outside the Church" doesn't exclude non-Christians from God's love. It merely repeats, in the sacramental mode, what Saint Peter said about Christ: "There is no salvation outside of Jesus." This doesn't mean that those who don't know Christ are doomed; it simply reminds us that God, in his benevolent design, instituted the Church as the sign of Jesus the Savior. To anyone who doesn't recognize this sign, one can say without being offensive: "There is no *recognized* salvation outside the Church." This nuance is thus an invitation to recognize this sign and not to exclude others from the reality of salvation.

Hence, in the absolute, it is always equally exact to say: "There is no salvation outside the Church," so long as one promptly adds: "This doesn't mean—in regard to people of goodwill outside the Church—that the Church has the monopoly on salvation; it simply means that the Church is the sign of salvation." The Church is Christ's servant and it can only be a sacrament if it humbles itself before Him. A useless and indispensable servant. Useless, because it is God who counts. Indispensable, because God counts on the Church. Wasn't it God who established the Church in Jesus Christ?

• God, the World, the Church.
1. *The Church Shapes the World*

Founded at the beginning, carried by a people's history, formed throughout this history, the Church was truly born by the act of Christ's death and resurrection and brought to the world at Pentecost. Thus, the world appears as the marvelous domain of creation, a gift of the Spirit. A domain that is God's property. A property that is not devoid of freedom. The world has its autonomy. It manages its affairs by its own lights. God and the world don't get in each other's way. The world has its own finality. It doesn't go against God's design, which is lyrically painted by Saint Paul in the first two chapters of the Letter to the Colossians and the first two chapters of the Letter to the Ephesians:

> Before the world was made, he chose us, chose us
>   in Christ. . . .
> He has let us know the mystery of his purpose,
> the hidden plan:
> that he would bring everything together under Christ,
>   as head,
> everything in the heavens and everything on earth.
>
> All things were created through him and for him.
> Before anything was created, he existed,
> And he holds all things in unity.
> Now the Church is his body,
> he is its head.
> He is the Beginning.

This vision, in which Christ's salvation seems taken for granted, radiates so much serenity that the supernatural seems natural. We already appear to have reached those peaceful times when the lion and the lamb lie down together. The Church incorporates the world, both of them gathered under one head: Christ.

Saint Paul then dares to say about the Church what he says about Christ. In the Letter to the Colossians, we find: "God wanted all *perfection* [fullness] to be found in him [Christ]" (Colossians 1:19).

And in his Letter to the Ephesians:

"[Christ is] the head of the Church, which is his body, the *fullness* of him who fills the whole creation" (Ephesians 1:22–23).

The Church appears as the bond between Christ and the world. The Church is not supposed to polarize the world; on the contrary, it has to efface itself in order to become the invisible bond that manifests the fullness, the perfection of Christ, "who fills the whole creation." The world is called upon to find this fullness in something greater than itself and the Church is *not* greater than itself. The world is called upon to look at him who is its Beginning, Christ Resurrected, the Pantocrator of our Romanesque basilicas. This focus inevitably crosses that of the Church, for the Mediation Church is located at the crossroad of this path to God. The Sacrament Church does not present itself as the goal to reach. It invites the world to go further than the world, further than the Church, to reach that invisible fullness and perfection.

The absolute invisible fullness of Christ is made visible by the sacramentality of the Church, which is fullness *relative* to Christ. The relationship between the World and the Church is set up in terms of that double dimension, both visible and invisible, which expresses the nature of the Sacrament Church only if we recall that a sacrament is a visible sign of an invisible reality. Before tackling this relationship between the World and the Church, it may be useful to remember that we shouldn't separate the visible from the invisible if it means reducing the Sacrament Church to nothing.

How often are we not tempted to oppose *visible* and *invisible*, as though the visible in the Church were the institution charged with all the sins on earth, and the invisible the communion filled with all grace. We forget all too frequently that the institution with its hierarchy and its structures is a gift of the Spirit. We don't see the share of grace in the opacity of the human. We forget that the invisible communion—a communion of saints, which is not a communion of the perfect—is itself charged with the secret weight of the sins of everyone.

2. The Church Exists before the World

If we agree that the Church's calling is to ask the world to find its fullness, its perfection, in Christ, we must then accept the fact that the Church existed before the world which it calls. In order to call someone, one doesn't stand in back of him. One projects one's voice to him. In these terms, one can state: the Church precedes the world.

It precedes it in time and space and on the level of Being according to which it is written: "In the beginning was the Word." (John 1:1) "All things were created through him and for him. . . . The Church is his body, he is its head" (Colossians 1:16–20).

"Do not believe," says Origen, "that the Church has existed only since the coming of the Savior in the flesh; the Church has existed since the beginning of the human race and even since the creation of the world (as vouchsafed by

Saint Paul). The first foundations of the Church were thus laid at the very beginning. This is why Saint Paul also says that the Church is founded not only on the apostles, but also on the prophets. Adam himself is counted among the prophets." The Church, which will visibly disappear with the world, remains eternal in Christ, whose word the Church has, whose Word it is. Father Lubac says: "In regard to both the Church and Christ, one must declare that both its reign and his reign will never end."

If we agree that the Church precedes the world, then we have to accept the corollary. From a pastoral viewpoint, there may be certain difficulties, since the absolute character of such an assertion may shock a Christian mentality trying to be respectful of the world. If we say that the Church precedes the world, we do not mean that the Church has precedence over the world. We do not mean that the Church has priority or superiority over the world. The Church is merely the sign of God's plan: to bring everything together under one head: Christ; to reconcile everything in Christ.

The Church doesn't have to adapt to the world, nor does it have to adapt the world to the Church. Its mission is to adapt the world to the world, to get it to find within itself the means of becoming what it must be. "As a servant of Jesus Christ and not of the world, the Church has the mission of attesting with its life the salvation plan that it announces, and of contesting, with this testimony of life, the world in its rejection of its own vocation" (Monsignor R. Coffy).

What proud audacity to say that the world is made for the Church rather than the Church for the world! What proud truth! The Church is faced, however, with the permanent temptation of confusing the visible and the invisible dimension and of recovering Christ's invisible primacy for the sake of its institutions and interests, thus forgetting his singularity with respect to the world. "The Church," says Monsignor Coffy, "is a sacrament only to the extent that it is different, that it is distinct from the world, so that questions may be asked." History bluntly attests that the Church has not always managed to escape its compromises with the world. How many times, indeed, has the Church availed itself of this primacy of the invisible that Christ entrusted to it not for itself, but for the world, the salvation of the world. How will the Church place itself in the relationship between God and world?

3. *What Church for What World?*

If we now try to make a rough survey of how the Church has placed itself with respect to the world throughout the centuries, we may schematically distinguish four phases:

· **The Age of Constantine, the Age of Christendom; Until the Church of Modern Times.**

The world and the Church are confused with each other. They form one entity in a spreading Christian civilization. This flood of Christian culture drowns the Gospel. The Church is more concerned with teaching doctrine and morality than announcing the risen Christ. It is then discovered, although a bit late, that the world of the baptized is not a Christian world. The Church goes to a lot of trouble to become smaller in scope.

Now for a big leap through history.

France, a Country with a Mission

The Church is a tiny remnant, a tiny nucleus that tries to burst and grow. Like any minority, the Church agitates. Now comes the colossal effort of Catholic Action (*Action Catholique*) and the Young Catholic Workers (*Jeunesse Ouvrière Catholique*) which sings: "We'll make our brothers Christians again!" And there are also the heroic labors of the worker priests. This is the pastoral way of many priests who, refusing to be locked up in regular worship, prefer (according to ecclesiastic jargon) "evangelizing over sacramentalizing." In this light, with the best intentions of the world, the Church once again brings everything back to itself rather than to Christ. It makes itself the center of the relationship between God and the World. According to the concept—God/Church/World—the Church still runs the risk of viewing itself as an end in itself. This is translated into the aggressiveness of a certain number of Christians who sigh about "the poor Church" and do everything they can to save it! They dare not admit—under cover of a missionary spirit—the old unconscious dream of finding a well-established Church again.

Yes indeed! Think of it! It's not unpleasant to belong to a Church with authority! How often do Christians want the Pope, the bishops to state their opinion on some topical issue, as though the Church as institution always had its official word to say about everything, as though Christians were incapable of embodying in their actions these discourses whose words sound good but change nothing.

The desire to have a Church that's presentable to the world is very praiseworthy. But doesn't it sometimes conceal the old unavowed dream of finding the good old Church of the past, the Church of a dear, departed Christendom, albeit a Church in clothes that have been retailored for the fashion of being open to the world?

The Era of the Council

The presence in the world and a dialogue with others have never been so fervently discussed as during Vatican II. This favorable outlook on the world is all to the credit of the Church. But the implied conception of the Church facing the world doesn't seem altogether satisfactory. For, on the pretext that it can't be reduced to the world, the Church is regarded as a foreign body. Yet the world and the Church are made of the same stuff. While the Spirit of the world may not always harmonize with the Spirit of the risen Christ in the world, the human realities experienced by the Christian are no different from those experienced by the non-Christian. The Christian has to cope with the same problems as the non-Christian. In the working world, he struggles with everyone else, like anyone else. In the social domain, he strives for change in the same ranks as others who do not share his so-called religious aspirations. In politics, he wages the same battle as so many others who have other options. And so on in other areas of life.

• The Era of the Diaspora

Our Church can no longer present itself to the world as an unassailable monolithic bloc, having its own worlds within the world. Nor can it even claim to be a chosen people. The Church is certainly the People of God. But a people that is not outside the world. A people that expresses its unity through the diversity of cultures and the pluralism of options. A people apart, to be sure, yet taking part in everything that makes up human life. A people who is not an arrogant and coagulated entity, but an uncountable multitude of men and women similar to others and different from others.

Our Church is the Church of Christians *dispersed* in the world and *gathered* in a community to celebrate living in the faith in Jesus Christ. Wherever they are, Christians receive the questions of Christians and non-Christians. The questions of faith are no different from the questions of everyone else's lives. So far as these questions of the world, experienced by Christians, refer to non-Christians, the Church makes a sign. This sign has the quality of an appeal, so that the question doesn't trail off into three dots but looms as a question mark of faith. At this point, one can speak of testiony, for the question becomes challenging speech, sacramental speech. We are no longer thinking of God/Church/World but God/World/Church. The latter sequence has the advantage of urging us never to forget that the fundamental relationship is the one between God and the World, and that the Church is here, sacramental, as the mediation of this relationship and not as the intermediary.

· A Point of No Return

It would, at the very least, be both childish and pretentious to make people think that our era is finally the good era, the era that has finally understood. It would be unfair not to recognize all the work done through the centuries to reach what Cardinal Marty calls the point of no return:

"Six years after the Council, we have reached the point of no return: the Church no longer has to ask itself whether it should go into the world. It *is* in the world. It carries within itself the confrontations and questions of all people. . . . The mission refers us today to the faithfulness of the Church, to its own identity, to the quality of the sign that it gives of itself. . . . The best service that the Church can render to the world is to be itself in this world. The mission thus refers us to Churchly life, to the holiness of Christians, to the quality of institutions. . . ."

5

Jesus: Someone to Adopt
Baptism

You have been taught that when we were baptized in Christ Jesus we were baptized in his death; in other words, when we were baptized we went into the tomb with him and joined him in death, so that as Christ was raised from the dead by the Father's glory, we too might live a new life.

In union with Christ we have imitated his death; we shall also imitate him in the resurrection. We must realize that our former selves have been crucified with him to destroy this sinful body and to free us from the slavery of sin. When a man dies, of course, he has finished with sin.

But we believe that having died with Christ we shall return to life with him: Christ as we know, having been raised from the dead will never die again. Death has no power over him any more. When he died, he died, once for all, to sin, so his life now is life with God; and in that way, you too must consider yourselves to be dead to sin but alive for God in Jesus Christ (Romans 6:3–11).

· The Newness of God

You're asked this question point-blank:

"What *new* thing has Christ brought into your life?"

What do you say? Do you recognize yourself in the following replies (randomly collected in numerous conversations and grouped in four categories that reveal four types of Christians)?

1. A teaching. A morality. A way of seeing life, of judging, of acting.

2. An ideal. A meaning to my life. A hope. Joy.

3. I don't know what new thing Christ has brought me, for I've always been a Christian. God is part of my habits, my ways of thinking. I just can't imagine what I'd be like if I hadn't been raised as a Christian.

4. I can't quite put into words what new thing Christ has brought me, but I feel it. What has he brought me? Everything! Strength and love in strength. He's given himself, and I believe I've given myself to him.

Yes, God so loved the world that he gave his Only Begotten Son. And we're so stodgy that we've become incapable of relishing the newness of such a revelation. And yet, if there's anything new in Christianity, it's this: God giving Himself. God never stops giving himself to each person in a unique way that's always new. Our God is the New-God. In this sense, Father Girardi writes in *Christianisme, libération humaine, lutte des classes*: "So, to him who asks us about *what new thing Christ has brought into our lives*, we have only only one answer to give: *Christ*. His truest and most transforming contribution isn't what he has given; but what he is, with the Father and the Holy Spirit. His newness isn't in the gifts he offers, but in the love by which he gives himself.

It is in this overwhelming experience of faith that the Christian grasps the creative impact of this Presence and this Love."

The day of the baptism in the Jordan, it was in these terms of Presence and Love that the Father presented Jesus to humanity:

> "This is my Beloved Son
> He has all my love."

That's all. The Father adds nothing else. He doesn't boast about what this exceptional son will do. He doesn't say what this wonderful son will bring. Baptism manifests this active presence of love with the same discretion. "Baptism manifests. . . ." doesn't mean that baptism proves the existence of God or demonstrates that Christians are right to believe. The word *manifest* shouldn't lead us to think that God makes us see clearly the new thing he brings to man. His message *is* clear, of course, but the way to live it is less clear.

Manifest really means: bring to light, expose the interior, make the light appear gradually to those who are in the proper conditions for perceiving it. In this sense, baptism invites man to seek perseveringly, to grope his way to the hidden presence of a Love that is not so evident. The light manifested by baptism is analagous to the light of a haze that slowly lifts, allowing us to hope for the fine weather we believe in . . . when the sun is here! While we wait for the light of faith, baptism says nothing. Or rather: it speaks only to those who hope. Baptism, the source of hope, is a sign of faith. A faith that mobilizes all the freedom of man touched by God.

Baptism makes a sign. It commits every human being to speak out in favor of God. It commits man to choose God. But you don't choose God haphazardly. The sheer freedom to choose God is itself a gift of God. God chose man first. God chose first to give man this gift of being able to choose. God, having chosen a people, reveals the way in which he likes to be chosen. Baptism, instituted by Jesus Christ, is the expression of this plan of God's and we have to approach baptism through its history.

Let us enter this area of the Revelation peacefully, beyond any pastoral controversies; not to eliminate thorny issues that pop up, but rather to provide them with a foundation. Having taken this pastoral viewpoint in my book on baptism (*Le Signe de la Foi*: Le Seuil, 1968), I tried to show that we can't discuss baptism theoretically when we talk to our contemporaries. Quite obviously, we can't ignore the missionary situation and speak about baptism as though ours were a world of Christendom. However, it is not through worldly choices that one can discover this joy of wanting to live authentically the eternal youth of God, signified by baptism. Instead, let's stand in awe of this radical innovation, which makes each of us new human beings, baptized in the name of the Father, the Son, and the Spirit....

· Baptism, an Institution of Jesus Christ
1. First Act of the Institution:
the History of the People of God

Christian baptism has a history. It has a life. It has a meaning. Its history is that of God's people, who, since its origins, has grown in understanding and acceptance of the story of Jesus Christ. The meaning of this history is the very life of Jesus Christ dead and resurrected. The life of the risen Christ is the meaning of the Church today. The Church remembering its roots. The Church fathers, especially Saint Gregory of Nyssa, tended to view the key episodes of the Old Testament story as announcements of Christian baptism. Thus, the water of creation, the water of the deluge, the water spurting from the rock at Meribah, the water of the Red Sea allowing the crossing—they all prefigure baptism.

2. Act Two of the Institution: the Rite of a Prophet

John the Baptist, the last prophet of the Old Testament and the first of the New Testament, the last prophetic figure of baptism becomes the first realization of Christian baptism. His baptism of water was a rite of penitence and purification, a call to conversion. Every good Jew who passed through the waters of the Jordan agreed to admit that he or she was a sinner. A sinner with hope because he or she was a sinner called upon to have a change of heart. By agreeing to receive the baptism of sinners, Jesus the Just manifests that his solidarity with human beings goes to the very limits of what a human being is. Even more! Because Jesus the Just plunges into human weakness—as the Son of God—he makes this obvious fact emerge: Man can get out of it. But not by himself. It is Jesus who saves. John the Baptist's baptism has an eschatological scope signifying the end of time which means that the end of time is not the end of the world, but the start of a New World, the inauguration of the saved World in this world. It is in this sense that we hear: "The last days are here. Time is at an end. The Kingdom of God is at hand" (Mark 1:14). For "He who is to come is coming. He is here." Thus, Isaiah's words come true: "All flesh will see the salvation of God" (Isaiah 3:6). All flesh will see the Sun!

What the evangelist records is not so much Jesus Christ's testimony of solidarity with sinners as the will to manifest: Who Jesus is: the Savior. Indeed, the Gospel says "It was to reveal him to Israel that I came baptizing with water" (John 1:31). And the presence of the Spirit, as a dove, attests that this water is not merely a symbol of purification, but a sign of the effusion of the Spirit himself.

To present baptism as a manifestation of salvation reveals that to be saved is not merely to feel inwardly that God is good and that his mercy wins out over sin. Naturally, faith makes us certain of salvation. However, this certainty could be just a subjective and individual impression. Baptism is an outward sign of the content of faith, because it is a sign God gives me that I have not invented. Revealed according to God's design and exposed in the Church, salvation is a truth that one experiences visibly with others and through others, within a people. Through baptism, Jesus Christ makes a sign to man. Jesus Christ invites man to recognize the way in which he, the Son of God, has committed himself to mankind. Baptism protects us against the mirage of looking for the Savior outside of what he is: Jesus Christ dead and resurrected.

To present baptism as a manifestation of salvation doesn't mean that we regard baptism as a sort of insignificant backdrop to faith. A sacrament has its own efficacy:

not to "produce grace" (what an awful way of putting it!),
but to be the site where God acts. God does not act in thin
air. Nor does a sacrament. God is committed to acting
through the mediation of the sign he has instituted. Each
sacrament shows the way in which God works on hearts in
the great moments of Christian existence throughout life.
Through all the sacraments, God's action, differentiated, is
fundamentally the same: it is always the power of the Spirit
bringing Jesus Christ back to life. Because baptism is the
sign of this action of the Spirit, every sacrament has a baptismal dimension. The Church itself, carrying out the sacraments, is essentially baptismal. Thus, when we say that
baptism manifests salvation, we are not saying that baptism
is content to teach us from the outside that God saves us. On
the contrary: we are affirming that God's action in resur-
recting Jesus Christ comes from the sacrament as a call from
God, giving each human being the strength to enter the
death and resurrection of Jesus Christ.

This is the power of the sacraments.

3. Act Three: The Sign of Fire and of the Spirit

John's baptism manifests that the Father and the
Spirit are recipients of the baptism of Jesus. Indeed, if baptism expresses the action of the Father resurrecting the Son
by the power of the Spirit, then baptism is necessarily trinitary; however, Jesus instituted this trinitary baptism in his
own name. The Acts of the Apostles report that the early
Church baptized "in the name of Jesus." It was not thereby
eliminating the Trinity; it was simply underscoring that the
institution of baptism does not merely come from a decision

of Christ's, it is rooted in the very life of Christ, who experienced and brought about what he commands us to do. The baptism he established was instituted by him in his death: "Can you drink the cup that I must drink, or be baptized with the baptism with which I must be baptized?" (Mark 10:28). Just as the institution of the Eucharist manifests the total gift of Christ's life, so too baptism manifests the passage from death to life, which embraced all of Christ's existence: "I have come to bring fire to the earth, and how I wish it were blazing already! There is a baptism I must still receive, and how great is my distress till it is over!" (Luke 12:49–50). Christ's link between the blazing fire and the baptism to be received even in distress leaves no doubt as to how Christ views the sacrament he instituted: he regards it as a passage from death to life. This is suggested by the symbolism of fire: it burns, destroys, wipes out, and transforms all matter so that something else may appear and so that life may be illuminated.

This mystery of death and life is the mystery of every Christian who identifies with Christ; it is also the mystery of the Church, the sacrament of Christ's body.

4. Act Four: The Institution, the Action of the Church

Baptism, instituted in the death and resurrection of Christ, commands every baptized person into the Church, which is instituted as a universal place of death and resurrection: "All authority in heaven and on earth has been given to me. Go, therefore, make disciples of all the nations; baptize them in the name of the Father and of the Son and of the Holy Spirit" (Matthew 28:18–19). The official institution of baptism appears as a flowering of the Easter mystery throughout the earth. Jesus doesn't say: "Make disciples of all nations by the love that you will live, by the charity that you will radiate, by the charisma that you will have, by the initiatives that you will take, by the faith to which you will bear witness." He says: "Baptize them."

To whom is Christ entrusting this mission? To the apostles. Yes, significantly and primarily to the Eleven, to whom he assigns this mission on the day of the Ascension. Jesus thereby explicitly emphasizes that he is communicating his authority as Christ the head to the apostles. "All authority has been given to me . . . . Go . . . . I am transferring it to you." Jesus founds the Church on the apostles. In the most immediate sense of the word, it is fundamental that the Church be apostolic. But baptism reveals that it would do no good to found an edifice without workers or material. As Saint Peter says, baptism makes every Christian a living stone that contributes to the construction of the whole. Baptism is what builds the Church. If all we had today was bishops, we'd have a Church of architects. It would be nothing but an open construction site, without workers or material. It is as valid to say that the Church makes baptism as that baptism makes the Church.

Through this sign of baptism, making all nations one nation, Jesus reveals his intention to create a place in which the Spirit can establish a type of relationship between God and man which is the sacramental structure of faith. To state that the Church was instituted in order to be instituting is, paradoxically, to emphasize that the Church as an institution has no other reason to exist than to be creative.

Creative modes of action by the Spirit—initiated by the Spirit himself—for the Church as an institution are a gift of the Spirit. Thus, when speaking about the Church as an institution, one is not boiling down the notion of institution to the ensemble of institutions of the Church. The Church as an institution is nothing but the Church as a sacrament, for an institution itself is a sign. The fundamental sign.

One demonstrates an infantile faith if one opposes the Church as an institution to the Church of the Spirit, as though the Spirit were alien to the institutional nature of the Church. As though the Spirit and an institution were opposites! On the other hand, one demonstrates a senile faith if one clings to out-of-date institutions by insisting on the primacy of the Church. The tragedy is that the institutions have the fearful power of killing the Church as an institution. There will always be a tension between the instituter and the instituted. Once the Church stops being an instituter in its institutions, it condemns itself to paralysis. This dialectic of the instituter and the instituted can be transcended only in the death and resurrection of Christ. For the Church, to live the death and resurrection of Christ is to kill the Church's human attachment to an established order that makes it the slave of its own constructions, in order to open up to the new creations of the Spirit. It is easy for the Church to verify its fidelity to the institution according to the Spirit. One of the immediate criteria is the vitality of prophecy. The instant the prophets are snuffed out in the Church and lose the power of speech, the institution is perverted. It serves something other than what Christ wanted it to be: the principle of an ever-living word for the world. If the Church no longer speaks to the world, then it is no longer faithful to what it is as an institution. Today, as we are forced to note, prophecy is fleeing outside the Church. Thus, I don't know the deeper reasons why Helder Camara did not speak to a synod that claimed to be talking about justice and peace in the world. There must be reasons that elude us; but one can't help feeling dismal about so much silence that kills the true prophets and gives rise to false ones. The false prophets exploit this situation, making themselves judges of the Church. At this point, it's useless declaring that prophecy is outside the Church; but we must acknowledge that this heresy of the Spirit is all too often provoked by those people who, within given situations, stifle the creativity of the institution. We would therefore, obviously, have to know who is a true and who a false prophet. A true prophet accredits his prophetic calling by the way in which he forgets himself, giving voice solely to love tested in humility. He proves he's a prophet when, freed from his own passions, he manifests nothing but the passion of Jesus Christ. If a prophet doesn't pass through death to himself in order to make the word of the Other, Jesus Christ, come forth, is he then a prophet inspired by the Spirit or merely a man who's tired of himself?

• Baptism: the Experience of the Passage

To say straight off that the Church as an institution is the will of the creative Spirit can only make one think that this truth out of a clear blue sky is something to take for granted. This consent to the Church as an institution is the immediate consequence of the baptismal character of our faith. Each time we deal with Christian life, the life of the

Church, in the light of Christ's life, we are brought back to the fundamental reality of baptismal life: the mystery of death and resurrection. To be both the Church as a sacrament and the Church as an institution simultaneously and indissolubly, the Church must simultaneously and indissolubly live the death and resurrection of Christ. We must therefore ask a question that I would like to call the question of the confidence of faith.

1. The Question of Confidence

Is it possible for man, such as he is constituted, to live what Jesus Christ lived for us? Saint Paul declares: "When we were baptized in Christ Jesus we were baptized in his death . . . so that as Christ was raised from the dead by the Father's glory, we too might live a new life" (Romans 6:3–4).

Are the realities that God asks us to live viable for man? I'm not talking about the exceptional man, the hero, the saint, but the average person, which is what all of us are. If the existential reality of our baptism is the identification of the risen Christ, will you then say: "I'd like to know how I can live in order to make my life this mystery of death and resurrection!"?

In what way does the Church teach us to die and rise from the dead? For centuries, the Church preached asceticism, conceived as a liberating death that makes the life of the Spirit germinate. In this, the Church relied on the testimony of God's life in the Gospels. We must, however, note that the evangelists don't say very much about any concrete asceticism of Jesus. They mention fasting, conceived as an emptiness, which will then be made good by God, who gives himself as nourishment: "Man does not live by bread alone, but by the Word . . ." (Deuteronomy 8:3). They also mention long vigils, that are understood as time given freely to God, for his glory. . . .

Jesus, no doubt, must have had lots of other ways to do penance. For instance, it's not written that his meals with sinners were loads of fun for him. The day he had a good lunch with Simon, Jesus might have preferred a good sandwich, eaten in peace and quiet . . . or nothing at all! Thus, it's neither the content nor the frequency of penitential acts that constitutes the true asceticism incarnating the death and resurrection of Christ. Naturally, all acts have their value, even an irreplaceable value; and by devaluating them, one eventually has to eat one's words. But, more fundamentally, it's the way in which all these acts are integrated in a unity of life, heading overall toward death and resurrection, that is significant to this mystery. One's whole life is a mystery of death and resurrection and not life sliced up into tiny, disconnected penitences.

How, then, can we actualize baptism in our existential lot, making our entire being, our entire acting, the experience of the death and resurrection of Christ? This question elicits another and more fundamental one, a question bearing upon what man is: Does the mystery of Christ's death and resurrection really connect to what we are in our heart of hearts? What does this mystery reveal to us about the human being that we are? When we examine the experience of Jesus Christ's life and then the human experience, we see that both are within a joint adventure: the adventure of a passage. Baptism, meaning, immersed, translates this experience of a passage.

The experience of a passage is the experience of God's people. It is the experience of Jesus Christ; it is also the experience of all human beings. It contains a human truth that can allow us to grasp which passage is meant in baptism. We will now turn to this exercise, which should crystalize what the word *passage* can evoke that is natural in human life and supernatural in baptismal life. We have to be able to examine ordinary everyday life and find a common link to baptismal life and life per se. The experience of the passage seems to constitute the structure of unity that permits us to make the link between faith and life.

2. The Cycle of Life

Whether it's day or night, winter or summer, whether God's creatures eat, sleep, or reproduce, the rhythm of nature is a perpetual movement from death to life. This rhythm is translated prosaically as the passage from light to dark, from destructive frost to rich harvests, from digestion to elimination, from sleeping to awaking, from childhood to old age. The rhythm of our natural environment reveals the internal rhythm of our lives, which are caught in the permanent tension that we feel within ourselves: between time and eternity, between the relative and the absolute, between the finite and the infinite.

Meant to live in the infinity of time, we are prisoners of passing time, and infinity eludes us in the immediacy of the moment. The words we use are revealing. Forever stalking time, we declare: "The lack of time is killing me." And if we happen to have time (when ill, when waiting), we are bored: "I'm killing time." Kill time and be killed by the lack of time: Isn't a death to oneself inscribed in this desire of ours to live fully? And all this without counting the trials of growing old. Just look at the frenzied way that Madison Avenue exploits the theme of rejuvenation. This fear of the corpse that we lug around inside ourselves day after day is posted on every wall and billboard. Death to oneself is carnally rooted in each person's core through this fury to live, which explodes everywhere and anywhere.

Meant to live in several places at once, we are condemned to being only where we are. All we do is leave and return: subway in the morning, subway at night, jammed highways, unjammed highways. Doesn't all this traffic in our earthly space concretely translate the movement of life to death and death to life? We perpetually have to double back. We have to pass from one point to another without ever possessing that towards which we are moving; isn't this too an elementary way of experiencing the passage from death to life?

Meant to encounter others, we go through all the disappointments of misunderstanding, the disillusions of love, the walls of incommunicability, the anguish of universal solitude.

3. Death and Love

At the end of this analysis, we could succumb to a temptation that I would like to call the temptation of the lid and the pot. Let me explain. Every day of our lives, we note a cycle of life and death. One might simply project this experience on to baptismal life, saying: It's the same thing in baptism! As though what we had to live in faith covered the content of our human experience, as though baptism were meant to consecrate a natural rhythm in nature and human life. Baptismal life does not put a lid on human experience; it goes through it, giving it substance and meaning. This radical inability to find the fullness we strive for, to realize eternity in an instant, infinity in the finite, the absolute in the fragment of the absolute that is a human life—this radical inability is death carved in the human heart.

It was no random choice of God's to pass through death in order to communicate love. He didn't just want to see the greatest of generosities through. His aim was to reveal the secret complicity between death and love. "To die of love" has always been the wild dream of ecstatic lovers. From Tristan and Isolde to the myth of the eternal return, this has been one of the great themes in world literature. Realizing that their love is greater than anything, greater than they themselves, they wish to live beyond themselves in that burst of death created by boundless communion. To establish God's communion with men, Jesus wanted to pass through death, in order to reveal to us that death and love have the same origin. Death per se is negative. It is a coming out of oneself that leads to nothing. Love is positive. It is a gift of oneself. Love is a coming out of oneself that changes everything. In death, the departure from oneself is pure nothingness. A wrenching away. A blotting out. In love, the departure from oneself is enriching. A transfiguration. A resurrection. In death as in love, one finds the same motion of departure from oneself, but with a different meaning.

To live life in a baptismal way is to fill the void constituted by death to oneself, to give it the content of love in such a way that the communion of Christ makes the fullness of life burst forth. In other words, when I say about baptismal life, "I am dying to myself," I am not resigned to just any death; I agree to die only for what Christ died for. It is not death for death's sake, but death out of love for life. This is the only death that's acceptable. Acceptable as a gift. For ultimately, to die to oneself as Christ died to himself is not appropriate to man. Baptism reveals that it's not natural to want to die to oneself. Only Jesus Christ can give me the right to die to myself as he died to himself. Baptism manifests to me that God can give me Jesus Christ's desire. The desire to die for love.

To enter into this baptism of Fire, to desire to die according to the Spirit, one must not flee life. Death to oneself is not suicide. It is life to the point of extreme lucidity. It demands not only giving what we have, but, above all, agreeing to offer what we do not have, what we are not. To offer one's death is to accept one's nothingness. To offer one's life is not only to give everything, but to give oneself too. Many Christians give a great deal of themselves. Do they give themselves like the Lord, who offered himself in person?

· Baptism, the Sacrament of Death and Resurrection

Perhaps we ought to recall that we won't die first and then rise from the dead. Death and resurrection are one and the same movement. It is by crossing death that resurrection comes instantaneously. True, there is a certain gap in the existential experience. Some days resemble Good Friday more than Easter. Some days can last a long time. On some days, we experience mainly death; on others, mainly the resurrection. This doesn't mean that there is a chronological order. The dichotomy that we can perceive in the course of days disappears when we view life as a whole. Human life is meaningless if not seen in its totality. Our life will have its full meaning the day of our death. But for now, to express the continuity of this unique act of death and resurrection, I would say: To die with Christ is to live, and to live with Christ is to die. To die to death in order to live to life . . . .

1. The Christian's Relationship to God Is Personal and Communal

The tattooed man is marked indelibly in his flesh. He has chosen a picture or word that says its say. The baptized man is tattooed by God, but he is marked on the inside. Baptism manifests that this mark is that of the risen Christ. Thus, when discussing the mystery of death and resurrection, we should never forget that we are talking about Christ. The Christian's resurrection is not some kind of spiritual power; it is Christ himself. This is what we sing at Easter. Christ is our Easter. Our Resurrection is Christ.

In the first approach, where the Christian experiences his personal relationship to Jesus Christ, we could state the following: If we make the death and resurrection of Jesus Christ ours, aren't we giving a positive meaning to anything that would be negative in life?

An example: Suffering is evil per se, a diminution of being. Hence, it is negative. Yet, in the communion with Christ's passion, can't it become God's compassion, establishing a universal sympathy with the world? It is thus a source of life-giving maturity, an intelligence greater than existence, a transcending. All life that thereby bursts out of passage from the negative to the positive is the resurrection in action. To make the mystery of death and resurrection ours through baptism is to give a new meaning to the most everyday human realities, to give them the density of hope that the resurrection carries within itself.

In the second approach, where the Christian experiences more fully his communal relationship to God, we can ask whether one might pass from the negative to the positive by orienting one's life towards the passage from the finite to the infinite, as with the risen Christ? Wouldn't this be giving our narrow lives the universal dimension that the eternal dimension of Christ gives to every created thing? We need to be persuaded that this universal dimension invisibly gives our lives an infinite breath; otherwise, we could easily wither in despair. Indeed, day by day, as we do whatever we can for peace and justice in the world, we sense more keenly our inability to change the course of things.

Isn't dying and being resurrected with Christ a triumph over this vertigo, whereby we assume the opacity of the human condition? Assuming one's limits does not mean resigning, much less rebelling; it means consenting to God's faint voice within us. For Christ is here, summoning us, hurling the words of Genesis at us, God's testament on the world: "Live and make life, increase and multiply, rule over the world...." Baptism reveals that God's collective testament given to the human community is also a testament addressed to each person individually. It is up to each person to make the world more livable, so that one day the world may become the new earth! Everybody, on a family level, a professional and political level, through a human action within his power, gives birth to the world in the cosmic birthpangs that Saint Paul talks about to the Romans (chapter eight). In revealing this collective and personal dimension of God's plan, baptism asks us to recognize sin and salvation in the world and in ourselves.

To die to the sin in the world is to refuse to exalt the world in a Babel-like way: Yes, God said to rule the world, but don't let the world rule us! The Christian is not a slave who submits to the world; nor is he a sorcerer's apprentice who makes himself master of the world. He recalls the Tower of Babel. To make politics something else, for instance, as though it were a required condition for faith, may be a Babel-like way of exalting the world. Likewise, abstaining from politics may be a way of scorning the world. Isn't it true that living the mystery of salvation means making the world be born to a new life by accepting the birthpangs in the finite world without seeing the outcome?

2. Baptismal Life Is Filial, Fraternal, Spiritual

One sees one's baptism as God sees baptism—but not because one has the sincere impression of dying to oneself when opening oneself up to a new life. To be recognized as truly baptismal, the experience of passing from death to life must be what Christ himself went through in his relationship to the Father and the Spirit. If we forget this trinitarian view of death and resurrection, we turn the Easter mystery into an ideology.

The baptized Christian is asked to live the death and resurrection of Christ not only within a human experience and a generous faith, but within a filial, fraternal, and spiritual relationship that is the human expression of God's transcendence.

Baptismal Faith Is Filial

It is because baptism identifies us with Jesus Christ, who alone is perfectly the Son, that we are certain of being viewed and loved by God as his children. Only Christ resurrected, "Firstborn of Creation," can extend this possibility of being the Son to all people on earth. Baptism is precisely the sacrament that manifests this power of Chist's to make each person filial. It is within this filial relationship of mankind to God that we are asked to incarnate the death and resurrection of Christ. For the Christian, dying and rising again is a filial act, the very act of Christ's love experienced in each human being. We would have to repeat everything we've said about situating ourselves with regard to the Father and about the transcendencies required of us to love as true children. But since we've already dealt with this issue, let's restrict ourselves to seeing in what sense we may argue that baptism makes us children of God. In what sense is God a father?

God can share his love with us only by making us his children, for He himself in the Spirit is fundamentally the Father who loves the Son. As God's children, we are thus related to his Son. It is the mystery of filial adoption, as revealed by Saint Paul in the Letter to the Galatians: "God sent his Son . . . to enable us to be adopted as sons . . . . The proof that you are sons is that God has sent the Spirit of his Son into our hearts: the Spirit that cries, 'Abba, Father,' and it is this that makes you a son, you are not a slave any more; and if God has made you son, then he has made you heir" (Galatians 4:4–6). Saint Paul's overemphasis on the truth of this filial relationship is repeated by Saint John: Think of the love that the Father has lavished on us, by letting us be called God's children; and that is truly what we are" (I John 3:1). Here again, John proves the need for emphasis by saying "truly." What does this *truly* mean? Colloquially, when we talk about adopted children, we know that even if they're marvelously loved by their adoptive parents, they are not theirs. Likewise, when Saint Paul declares that we are God's sons, we fully realize that Jesus Christ alone is God's only Begotten Son, not made but begotten. He alone can bear this name, which is above any other name. *We*, however, are God's *adopted* children.

But there's a concrete difference between human adoption and adoption by God. The adopted child can't say he was born of his adoptive parents; but the Christian *can* say, not as an image, but in all truth, that he was born of God. This birth is the "new birth" through Jesus Christ resurrected (Ephesians 1:5); baptism is the sign of this new birth, which Jesus announced to Nicodemus: "Unless a man is born from above he cannot see the kingdom of God" (John 3:3). It is because we are likened to him who is the Only Begotten Son resurrected—who is truly re-born—that we can speak about ourselves as being reborn. This adoption as children is not outside ourselves. It is part of our very being. Baptism is the official act of recognizing our adoption as children. It stamps on us a way of being filial.

The revelation of this filial adoption asks Christians to live in the freshness that Claudel mystically calls "the eternal childhood of God."

To be fathered by God, to father God in ourselves—such are the dynamics of the growth of faith in every human heart: we must both let God adopt us and adopt God throughout our lives. This adoption endlessly presupposes choices. Indeed, faith banishes routine. It is the election of love. "It is not you who chose me," say Christ, "I was first . . ." (John 15:16). Yes, but if God first chose man, man is called upon to choose God as the first.

Faith is irreconcilable with conformism. One doesn't believe automatically. Faith, the fruit of the living tradition, is a heritage that Christian families pass on to their children. But this doesn't mean the heritage is systematic. It too necessitates a choice, an acceptance. One can refuse a heritage. Which is something we see so frequently nowadays. Children reaching majority disinherit themselves. They reject the religion bequeathed by their parents, not only the trivial knickknacks of an insipid faith, but also, alas, the lovely hidden values of a faith they have never discovered. And yet, the baptism of babies paradoxically reveals the adultness of faith. Baptism fools neither the child nor the parents. Since the pastoral news of baptism, parents are more aware that the child, baptized at their request, must some day personally confirm this choice and be confirmed in the Spirit.

This spirit is that of the Pentecost manifesting the adulthood of the total man achieved in the resurrected Christ in whom resides the fullness manifested by the Sacrament Church. This Spirit is also that of Christ's childhood. The Spirit of childhood spoken of in the Gospel has the frailty and strength of God. Frailty, because God surrenders frankly to man. He abandons himself in innocence to the love of man, in whom he believes. Strength because in man's lost innocence, God gives man the fortunate chance to become and rebecome a child, the child of God.

Baptismal Faith Is Fraternal

It's because baptism identifies us with him who lived with all men as as universal brother that we are certain we can regard every living human being as a brother. Only Christ, the eldest of a multitude, can extend the power of viewing one's neighbor as a brother to all people on earth. Baptism is precisely the sacrament that manifests Christ's power to make every human being fraternal. It is also within this fraternal relationship that we are asked to incarnate Christ's death and resurrection, that is, to live love as in the Easter mystery. Charity, indeed, is not a virtue of kindness; it is the way to love as Jesus Christ dead and resurrected loved. It is the expression of the death and resurrection. The hymn to charity sung by Saint Paul in the Letter to the Corinthians might seem like a list of moral admonitions to be charitable: charity is patient, it's not envious, it's not puffed up with pride, and so on.

Actually, these aren't bits of advice so much as those revealing traits of the love that Christ lived personally in his death and resurrection.

Baptismal Is Spiritual Faith

When I say that baptismal faith is spiritual, I mean that Christian faith is universal. Why? Because the Spirit of Jesus resurrected has the power to universalize everything. The relationship to the Father makes us sons. The relationship to the Son makes us brothers. The relationship to the

Spirit makes us universal. What the risen Christ does in every human being, he does for all humanity, gathering it in one body, one people. One may therefore say that because Christian faith comes from the Spirit, it is universal, i.e. it addresses all of a person, everyone, all mankind. There's another way of expressing this universal character of faith; i.e. by saying faith is of the Church. Because the Church is the universal sign of the Spirit inviting the world to form one body, Christian faith can be lived only within the Church, in the God/World relationship that we have discussed.

Every baptized Christian is thus asked to live personally the mystery of the death and resurrection that the Church lives as a whole throughout the world. There is, I feel, one criterion among the criteria that allow us to test the authenticity of this death to oneself that must be assumed. I am referring to the capacity to stay in the Church when so many things could make one either slam the door or tiptoe out. Baptism, the sign of faith, manifests the fact that one can fully live an adult faith only by staying attached to the Church. However, certain Christians may have conscientiously broken this bond, at least for a while. To live one's baptism in the heart of the Church is to place oneself in a state of reform, that is, a state of death in order to come back to life again. This consists not in judging those who now desert, but rather in acting in such a manner that some day perhaps these prodigal Christians could recognize themselves as belonging to the Church through those who remain. This lucid faithfulness, assuming the limits of the Church and also rejecting escape, is one way to live death to oneself so that Christ may live.

By way of a test, to sharpen the practical sense of people who desire something concrete, allow me to ask a few very simple questions. What do you consider most important? The liturgical details that can change and that annoy you? The style of certain priests whom you judge from the outside? The structures, the pastoral options, etc.? Or else, the fact that hope no longer buds in the world? Just what is the Good News anyway? If we're consumed by our problems and also disengaged from the world, we may no more be within the Church than those who leave it. Might not the passage from death to life consist in knowing how to renounce one face of the Church, which we clutch tooth and nail, and to accept the Church's birth in the world beyond our options and opinions?

· The New Human Being

Baptism, thus understood as the revelation of Jesus Christ living his death and resurrection today in each one of us, throughout the world, commands us to remember him at all times and in all ways. This means that baptism essentially orders us to celebrate the memorial Eucharist of the death and resurrection of Christ. All Christian life is a Eucharist in the sense that the Eucharist permanently actualizes the mystery of faith in the action of the Spirit's grace. I thus spontaneously feel rising within me Mary Magdalen's song in *Jesus Christ Superstar*. It is the song of the New Human Being:

"Lord, I exist for you."

What better way to exalt the action of baptismal grace

that is the entire Eucharist than to celebrate life as a reference to the Other?

The baptismal commitment celebrated in the Eucharist is a double reference:

"God, by becoming flesh, lives for man and—man, by incarnating God in his life, lives for God.

God gives himself to man according to a mode of sacramental presence, because he lives for man. . . . Man agrees to receive baptism in order to meet God according to the mode of presence he reveals, because he lives for God.

We now have to ask how each of our days string together with the others to form the great life of God's children: do we permit God to exist in us?

> Lord,
> you know me.
> You know how far I go.
> I've given a lot
>   my life!
>   my love!
>   my days!
> I've given everything
> Have I given: me?
> Have I given myself
>   my whole self
>   to be lived by you!

— 6

Jesus: Someone to Love

God as Love

My dear people,
let us love one another
since love comes from God
and everyone who loved is begotten by God and
knows God.
Anyone who fails to love can never have known
God,
because God is love.
God's love for us was revealed
when God sent into the world his only Son
so that we could have life through him;
this is the love I mean:
not our love for God,
but God's love for us when he sent his Son
to be the sacrifice that takes our sins away.
My dear people,
since God has loved us so much,
we too should love one another.
No one has ever seen God;

but as long as we love one another
God will live in us
and his love will be complete in us.

(First Letter of Saint John 4:7–12)

• Tell Me: Which Love Is Meant?

Love! Christians are rebuked for having only this word on their lips. Granted, since they talk of love in regard to everything and nothing, one can no longer tell what love they're talking about. To hear certain Christians speak of charity so harshly and sometimes so violently, we wonder which love they love. By repeating frivolously—and quite generously, no doubt—"everyone who loves is begotten by God," one ultimately sets up any old love as godly. What a subtle temptation to make an idol of love! Is love all we need to claim we are God's? Is claiming we're God's all we need to claim to love? I'm generous, I'm nice to others, I'm not a racist, I love others—but does all this make me God's?

• Love Is a Revelation
The Morality of Love

Human love derives from different feelings, depending on the situation. When I love my father and mother, my brothers and sisters, my spouse, it's the same thing . . . and not the same thing! When I love out of natural lovingness or when I charitably love a person whom I forgive, I always love with the same heart, for love is always love; but the motives differ. When a Frenchman loves a North African in the joy of being consistent with the love that Christ manifests for strangers, the evangelical content of this love is different from that which I have in my heart when I love a friend. Love is vaster than emotional spontaneity. Love is also the spirit that animates the feelings and the will to love in every heart. A will not in the voluntarist sense. A will in the sense of a power that activates all the faculties for loving: sensitivity as well as intelligence evangelized by the Love of Christ. Thus the occasionally used expression "to love out of charity" points out its specific redundancy: to love out of charity is to love out of love—the common ground between human love and divine love. Without going into the classical Greek distinctions between *eros* and *agape* or the theological distinctions between nature and grace, one can easily recognize that there is a unity between man's love and God's love, yet a difference.

To love another quite simply, to love God quite simply is not necessarily to love as God loves. For man, loving as God loves doesn't mean being like God. In this love, God is not reduced to man. Man does not become God. Faith is this communion of man with God, but a communion that respects the identity of each. One can only say: "Whoever loves expresses something of God." God's love in man's heart is not just any love. Human love presupposes a certain harmony with what God is and what he reveals to us of himself in the morality of love.

Morality of love? What would a morality be if it is not a morality of love? Perhaps we're disturbed: we note, for instance, that many love experiences can occur in a way that doesn't conform to the principles of morality. Can't love be experienced truly and beautifully in a situation that is judged to be immoral and abnormal? Many of the love stories we know come from situations in which two people live in a beautiful love, while, conjugally speaking, they are unfaithful to their mates. Who can dare to claim that their love is not love? And if their love is love, who can say that their love is not of God? Yet if it is not of God, is it truly love? Can there be true love without morality? Can there be a morality that disregards love outside the norms? This is a serious question. We are not trying to oppose morality to love, much less regard morality as a set of principles of decency that are exterior to man. Morality is the expression of man's truth, his faithfulness. Morality reveals man to himself. It teaches man to know himself and to surpass himself. But what does morality know about man? The more mysterious and perplexing the inner man, the more humble and the more human our morality must be, the less sectarian it must be.

If two people can truly know authentic love in an irregular situation—for instance, two lovers in what is conventionally termed living in sin, might not this love, which is seemingly marked by sin, be marked equally by salvation? Whatever the failures of human life, if someone, assuming the difficulty of his situation, acknowledges that his love has something both lost and saved in it, isn't it therefore situated in the light of Christ dead and resurrected? If, in the powerlessness of suffering, he is unable to escape and lives his suffering as a death to himself, then perhaps something of God passes through this death. Yet how can one remain true in a double life?

To maintain such an equilibrium of truth in life, one must obviously have absolute loyalty and, as Saint Luke, says, endlessly look to see whether the light within one is not darkness, and, finally, know what love one is speaking of. Between the Jansenism of long ago and the easy laxity of now, each person has to make his truth, his own truth that tends towards *the* truth. Between *my* truth and God's truth, there is Jesus Christ dead and resurrected. One is not excommunicated from God's love just because one doesn't succeed in loving as God loves. To the extent that one really dies to oneself in an "impure" love, there is bound to be something of "Pure-God" that is born. But the point is to die in order to live. Isn't this the essence of baptismal life revealed by Jesus as a mystery of re-creation? One can't be God's without being reborn. One can't love according to God without becoming a new creature. The key that opens the mystery of this life of love according to God is the mystery of death and resurrection that Saint John puts in these terms: "Everyone who loves is *begotten* by God."

At first sight, apparently, Saint John makes it seem as if love is all it takes to be God's. But when we illuminate this verse with others, a new light appears: Thus, in his first letter, Saint John says: "Anyone ... begotten by God has already overcome the world" (1 John 5:4). *Anyone begotten . . . .* Isn't there something like a restriction here, which might lead us to think that certain things are not born of God? Notice, he doesn't say: "Everyone who loves is God's," but "Everyone who loves is begotten by God. This little "begotten" is decisive. John is the only evangelist to state that one must be reborn in order to be God's. But it's certainly no coincidence that John emphasizes the need for a new birth if someone wants to love in the way God wishes. "Do not be surprised when I say: You must be born from above" (John 3:7). The words Christ spoke to Nicodemus reveal that this birth to a new life is a gift from God. It's God who gives us the ability to love as he alone can love. But how can we love this unseen God?

Embracing God

God's love leaves so many people cold—people who are thirsty for the absolute. We see that money, ambition, worldliness leave man perfectly alien to God. In the light of all this, we wonder how we can hope that modern man can love this God of Love who doesn't touch the worldly world. People think they've said the last word when they state peremptorily: "God isn't an ideology, but a living person!" Granted. But where is he? How can we hang out with God? We can naively say, "God isn't an idea, he's someone." But that doesn't make it any easier to get in contact with him. He eludes our sensibility; how can we embrace God with our entire lives?

We spontaneously refer to our experiences of human relations. The way people communicate with one another lets us perceive something of the mystery of man's communication with God. But only something! On the one hand, this interhuman communication is imperfect; and on the other hand, when we compare the mode of human relations with what could be the mode of man's relation to God, we notice that, despite several common points, there are, above all, huge differences. We then say that man's relation to God is analogous to what we know of human relations. Analogous means similar points, but also differences so great that one can't compare as with a carbon copy. The essential difference between the mode of man's relation to God and the mode of interhuman relations is simple: You don't see God, you can't touch him. "Perceptible to the heart," by all means. But you've got to renounce perceptibility if you want to meet him.

Thus, it's paradoxical to define faith as a relationship with God as a living person, if this person eludes our senses.... Paradoxical too in the sense that the road towards meeting God seems to reverse the order of what happens when two human beings discover one another. Let's take an engaged couple. It's after going through the stage of irresistible attraction to the woman he loves that a man can consecrate his choice once and for all and declare: "I give thee my troth." In other words, "I go beyond the selfishness of my passion, I get out of myself, I love you for yourself. I trust you." I can now say: "I believe in you." In his quest for God, the believer follows a reverse path. He usually has to get past the stage of a certain indifference before being able to say to God: "I love you." Hence, the believer must first say: "I believe in you," in order to discover the contents of the words "I love you."

It's after declaring his faith in God that the Christian can experience in love that which made Saint Paul say: "I know whom I have believed." Since God loves us first, definitively, one should perhaps simply let God love us. One should perhaps love the fact that God loves us and let well enough alone! Too many Christians are cramped; they won't let well enough alone. They fail to realize that they don't love the fact that God loves them. Or, even more simply, they fail to find in the Revelation with a capital R (which strikes them as cold), a revelation that enters their immediate lives with warmth.

A Dual Love

While expecting so much of love, we may be disappointed by the legalistic and moralizing aspect of the demands of love presented in the New Testament. What's it all about? Doesn't the beloved apostle, Saint John himself, have anything more exciting to tell us than to observe the commandments? And what about Saint Paul in his famous hymn to charity, which no one could dare not call a masterpiece? Doesn't he have anything better to offer than an inventory of banalities to practice? You don't have to be Saint Paul to tell us that "love is patient, it doesn't get angry, it's not envious." All well and good; but you need just a little experience to discover these things on your own. What, then, is this love all about?

The commandments Saint John speaks of are merely the expression of the new commandment: "Love one another as I have loved you." This commandment is not only a set of rules to observe, but a fidelity to discover and a freedom to create. Create what we are, according to what others are, according to what God is in the ardent communion that Saint John speaks of in terms of sharing and exchanging.

The concrete demands of love as stressed by Saint Paul are not so much advice or moral admonition as the very features of the face of Christ resurrected. Saint Paul doesn't paint a picture of things to practice. He draws a portrait of Christ as Love. This love brings grace, truth, service, forgiveness; it presupposes a slow death to oneself in order to welcome the purity of Christ into oneself. And if there is anything extraordinary about this description of love, it is the concrete verification of the love of faithfulness that Christ himself experienced to the very end

Through both Saint John and Saint Paul, the Revelation ultimately preaches nothing but faithfulness: love becomes flesh; love proves itself. It is only in such realism that we can state: "Everyone who dwells within love dwells within God."

The source of this faithfulness is not the law, sterile in itself; its source is Christ. The standard of this faithfulness is not the law; it is Christ, for man was not made for the law, the law was made for man. The only Christian reference for faithfulness is the person of Christ, who incarnates in himself the demands of Love. This is what Christ attempts to explain to the jurist of the Gospel who asks him: "What does a man have to do to have eternal life?" (Matthew 19:16). To this man of the law, Christ finds nothing to reply but a quotation from the Old Testament: "You will love the Lord your God with all your heart, with all your soul, and with all your might, and you will love your neighbor as yourself" (Leviticus 19:18; Deuteronomy 6:5). But one must smash through the already very wide framework of this life by situating it in direct reference to oneself. Jesus dares to present himself as the standard of all love. "Love one another *as I* have loved you, *as I* love my Father." This is what is so new.

God's love and man's love do not make a crowd: you don't love God *and* your neighbor, you love God through your neighbor. You love God for God's sake by loving your neighbor for your neighbor's sake. You love God for himself in your neighbor. You love your neighbors for themselves in God. This is the inextricable, dual love. How can we speak of this love?

· Tenderness Above All

Try It...

Who can speak of love if not the God of Love? However, when he speaks about it, he doesn't necessarily say extraordinary things. What's so extraordinary about it? The fact that he lives what he says. And what he lived among men, in the heart of history, he keeps on living today. Try tenderness and you will be seized with the love that one meets throughout the Revelation. How can we forget the words with which the prophet Hosea expresses the bonds of affection between God and his people, like those between a father and his beloved son: "I led them with reins of kindness, with leading strings of love" (Hosea 11:4).

This tenderness is untiring. Throughout the ups and downs of this stiff-necked people, the Lord says through Jeremiah and all the others: "Is Ephraim, then, so dear a son to me, a child so favored, that after each threat of mine, I must still remember him, still be deeply moved for him, and let my tenderness yearn over him?" (Jeremiah 31:20).

The tenderness is always there, even in the most difficult moments. In the time of ordeal in the desert of Exodus, when God is very angry, he finds a way to work a tender miracle—an unexpected menu: quails and manna!... This recalls classic family scenes: the child is impossible. The mother is at the end of her rope. She'll tell Dad when he comes home in the evening. And Dad will punish him by taking away his dessert. Mom will then secretly bring him something sweet.... Dad will know.... This secret complicity of love is what tenderness is all about.

In the Gospel, Christ manifests it in many ways:

He lets the children come to him:
　Yet he had other duties!
He lets the beloved disciple rest his head:
　Was this dignified?
He lets Mary Magdalen perfume his feet:
　He ought to be ashamed!
He lets the woman of Samaria tell her life story:
　What does this look like?
He lets the adulterous woman look at him:
　You can see what people might have said!

What Would You Say?

God's tenderness does not follow human manners. It is at ease in the heart of the tenderness of people as they are. In this respect, a rather curious feature comes out. The risen Christ appears first to those who loved with their hearts. The women. Yes, it's interesting to note that Christ first showed himself not to the apostles, but to Mary Magdalen and her companions, who then, like prophets of love, went to announce the great news to the disciples. This doesn't mean that males don't love with their hearts or that tenderness is a sign of weakness, a female prerogative. If women seem to have greater need for tenderness, perhaps it's because they're better at giving it!

Tenderness is love that knows how to give, love that knows how to receive. Tenderness won't be tied up in a definition. If you were asked to define a summer morning breeze, what would you say? A shiver? A caress? You can see this is no definition. If you had to talk about the unconscious beauty of islands that don't realize they're the queens of the earth and the sea, what would you say? And what about the soft steps of a mother and father entering the room where a baby sleeps? That's tenderness. Love's respect for things you touch only with your eyes. That's tenderness. Tenderness is within love, the way poetry is within things. Tenderness is the gentleness of love, the clear center. This is not extraneous, not an added quality; it's love.

A Penny's Worth of Tenderness

So give yourself a penny's worth of tenderness. Put two cents' worth of tenderness in your relations with others, and you'll discover that fidelity to the commandments, which may seem cold, is not just conformity to a law that must be applied, but the flowering of the freedom of the heart, which finds the true attitudes of love.

Put two cents' worth of tenderness in your relationship with God and you'll discover more vividly that faith is a dialogue of love. "Everyone who loves me, I will love him and manifest myself to him" (John 14:22). This is a veritable declaration of love that God makes to each of us. He says: "I love you." Isn't it wonderful that God wants to say no more than what man himself says when he can't say any more? When you say "I love you" from the bottom of your heart, the words remain in your throat. Tenderness is whispering. Or better, the silent desire of love.

So, finally, put an ounce of tenderness in your prayers, and though you may think you don't know how to pray anymore, don't like to pray anymore, you'll discover that with a little tenderness you'll pray the way you keep humming a song that you like. You don't know the words but you recompose the tune in major or minor, according to the moment.

Tenderness is the genius of love; it always keeps improving. Tenderness gives the silence between people the strength of intuitive communication.

Tenderness gives words between people the accent of love.

Tenderness gives to gestures between people the meaning of the unspoken.

Let's live in the power of tenderness. Let's experience love. God might then sing in our hearts: "Don't talk to me too much about love . . . but, at least from time to time, say tender things to me!"

> God
> I love you
> without even
> knowing who you are.
> I love you.
> We cannot seek you
> without loving.

> God
> I love you
> and I don't quite know what I'm saying
> and I don't quite know what I'm living
> but I know that I live
> and that living
> is loving you.

> God
> I love you
> and it's true
> that I don't know how to love.
> In this poverty of love
> I love you more.

Christ
I love you.
You let me love
as no one has ever loved
You let me love the Other
as you have always loved him.

From *L'espace d'un moment*,
by Pierre Talec.
Paris: Le Centurion, 1972.

— 7

Jesus: Someone to Speak to

Believe me, woman, the hour is coming
when you will worship the Father
neither on this mountain nor in Jerusalem.
You worship what you do not know;
we worship what we do know;
for salvation comes from the Jews.
But the hour will come—in fact it is here already—
when true worshipers will worship the Father
in spirit and truth;
that is the kind of worshiper
the Father wants.
God is spirit,
and those who worship
must worship in spirit and truth. (John 4:21–24)

· The Fragile Anemone

Throughout these chapters, as we have been in quest of the Resurrected, we have been constantly brought back to the Gospel, our source. There, we have found clear answers. Faith is God's life flowing into the heart of human life. The sacraments of the Church manifest this unity of the unique stream of faith and life.

This flowing stream is prayer. In the privacy of the heart or in a huge assembly, in all tones prayer sings the incessant celebration of the Sacrament Church over the world. Let us hollow our hearts and our minds like cupped hands to receive more effectively this living water.

Francis of Assisi said: "Love is no longer loved." Every century has many ways of deserting love. If anemia is characterized by thin blood, then the shortness of breath suffered by prayer today is a sign of anemia in our age. Prayer is the opposite of anemia. It is an anemone. In Greek, *anemos* is breath. Wind. Prayer is this fragile flower exposed to the great wind of love. A tiny flower so light in the air that it becomes the wind. It becomes the other. Prayer is becoming the Other. Becoming breath. Being taken by the Spirit. "The wind blows where it wishes. We do not know where it comes from, where it goes" (John 3:8). Prayer is ungraspable, a puff of the soul. Prayer aspires to love. Love inspires prayer. Love is free. Prayer celebrates freedom. It is not made to serve anything. It is. A smile heard from man to God.

To bathe prayer in this light of love immediately makes my words clear. Don't expect a plea for prayer here, as though the priest, an advocate of his cause, had to justify the existence of prayer, convince us of its necessity, recall its commandment. Seek love in any way, and prayer will be given to you in the bargain. Prayer is an act of love. Prayer is an act of faith. Love and faith are at stake here. Thus the weight of the question asked by prayer for a secular world far surpasses the future of liturgy. At stake is the future of mankind. The future of the world. The future of the Church. If prayer vanished from the face of the earth, what would mankind be with no interior life, the world with no chance of appeal, the Church with no communion?

· Prayer for a Disenchanted World
Praying out of Love

Prayer doesn't escape that jolt of controversy now shaking the body of the Church.

—*In its principle*, in its very being, prayer is being run down by an intellectualist movement wearing the boots—so often resoled—of our grandfathers, Nietzsche, Feuerbach, Engels: "Prayer is an alienation. A refuge for people who are scared of life. A house of cards for people who are schizoid about life. A drug. In sum, an escape."

Admittedly, Christians lay themselves open to this criticism. Hence, the claim that prayer is cowardly is a bias of those who judge it from the outside, through caricatures that are easy to poke fun at. One must truly never have prayed to imagine prayer as an escape hatch. The praying man knows that prayer is a presence to oneself, to others, to God. Prayer is reception and introspection. An assimilation that is terribly demanding, terribly trying, terribly committing; for in prayer, God's revelation of himself through words is confronted with his revelation of himself through life. It may then seem as if God is sometimes contradicted by the realities of life. The reality that God reveals and the realities that man perceives are two different things. Blessedness and happiness do not necessarily go hand in hand.

Thus, it appears that a new vision of the world is born in

prayer. God refers man back to himself. The Christian knows that you can't act in the same way after praying about a situation. You can't look at a person in the same way when you've prayed out of love, or, if you prefer, when you've loved in a praying way. Prayer may widen the human heart, but it is more often filled with wilderness. Dryness. Asceticism. A test of truth. We are far from alienation.

—*In practice*, people who no longer wish to pray are unimpressed by intellectual objections. The reasons for disaffection from prayer are more prosaic. They are tied to the contingencies of concrete life, which have been the same for centuries (nothing new under the sun): lack of time, fatigue, boredom. However, today, we must recognize that the conditions of urban life accentuate the difficulties: overcrowding, haste, noise, more and more distractions: TV, sexual promiscuity, etc. These are serious obstacles; but, strictly speaking, they are not fundamental objections. The stumbling block is not so much prayer itself as the disenchanted world. This was said by Weber. Disenchantment expresses what we call the desacralization of the universe.

The Church in a Demythologized Era

From all the control towers in the universe, scientists and philosophers, theologians of death, now surpassed by the theologians of the life of God, are announcing the great passage from a sacralized era to a demythologized era. Everything's been said about this topic. In great battles of words. This is not the place to venture into the labyrinth of subtle analyses. For the sheer goal of situating the prayer of secularized man, we must try to stake off our airstrip and put up a few approach lights. First of all, we have to get beyond the traditional opposition between the sacred and the profane, as though the sacred belonged to a reserved area—the gridded area of religion, of the supernatural—and the profane were nothing but the field of the poor natural world! Isn't life natural? And yet it's sacred! Isn't love natural? And yet it's sacred! Truth and peace are sacred. Everything coming from man is sacred; the whole world comes from man, hence it's sacred. That's the great discovery of secularized man. In *Man's Liberation* (*Liberation de l'homme*), Bernard Besret says: "God, in freeing us by the revelation of a sacral vision of the world, also frees us from a certain form of religion and of prayer tied to that vision."

Secularized man is man fully responsible for the world in this century. He keeps acquiring a greater and greater mastery over nature, revealing his own autonomy to him. He doesn't need to pray to God for results that depend on man. Science is atheistic by hypothesis; not because it rejects God, but because, by its methodology, it rejects a God of perpetual recourse, a God who can always help man, as though man had not been created big enough. Secularized man rejects a God who doesn't stay in his place, an intruder God who intervenes on the level of secondary causes, whose conduct belongs to man.

If Christian prayer makes it seem that man addresses God as a deus ex machina, then it becomes intolerable. Thus, the prayer of Rogation Days no longer passes muster in contemporary mentality. Our God isn't a God who makes rain and fine weather. To ask for God's protection is not to agree in a servile way with the favors of a frightening God; it means acknowledging that we can trust the creative freedom that God gives us.

So don't imagine that the secularized Christian is irreligious. Religion is the rope that ties man to God. What the secularized Christian contests is not the rope, but the splice in the rope. In other words, the secularized Christian rejects not a relationship of dependence on God the creator, but rather living in this relationship within the obscurantism of a mythology that makes the created world appear to have no consistence in itself.

Desacralization Is Not Profanation

Desacralization is absolutely not the death of God, it is a cleansing of idolatry from the heart of religion. Desacralization is not profanation. It is, to a slight degree, the great wrath of Moses coming down from Mount Sinai and fulminating against the golden calves. During the Exodus, the Jews replaced God with idols. For centuries now, something far more serious has occurred: we have used God's name to remake God in our image. Desacralization is a holy wrath. It has to be animated by Christ's great desire to make every man his house of prayer, every heart the temple of his Spirit. Desacralization is a difficult undertaking; for, on the pretext of exorcising a certain number of evil geniuses from religion, the secularized Christian risks creating a vacuum and finding himself in the house spoken of in the Gospel: a house that's been freed of demons, cleaned and well swept, but secularized (Matthew 12:43–45). Purifying isn't purging.

Thus, how can we today "worship in spirit and in truth"

according to Christ's wish? It seems that we are asked to find the road of transcendence again. But ever since God made himself human in Jesus Christ, we've known that transcendence is not beyond or outside mankind, it's in the hearts of men; for our God is also the Creator.

Paul VI reminded us of this in his letter to Cardinal Roy in 1971: "Christian faith . . . recognizes God, the transcendent creator who, through all the levels of the created, calls to man as responsible in freedom" (no. 27). Because God the Creator committed himself in creation by becoming a "creature" in Jesus Christ, "Firstborn of Creation," God has always been Emmanuel. He did not wait for the Nativity to reveal this. The entire Old Testament is filled with the interventions of "God with us." Thus, the God of Sinai in the splendor of his glory comes down from the mountain to enter into the black swamp of human freedoms. Christ was then able to make the woman of Samaria understand that it's wrong to seek places of prayer on mountain tops and in man-made temples. For God the Creator is the Spirit, and "those who worship" must create their worship "in spirit and in truth." The prayer of the secularized Christian is characterized by this quest for a God as Spirit and Creator who made himself human. A spiritual God who became flesh: here, we are far from the Oriental spiritualisms which, to find God, aim at a certain disincarnation. We are far from Hinduism, which doesn't know worship in the strict sense, for it tends to identify man with God. Worship presumes a distinction between man and God. Christianity, in the communion of the divine and the human, teaches us that Christ, himself distinct from his Father faced his father. To Abraham, God said: Remain in my presence.

I say these things because at the moment, non-Christian prayer forms have become faddish, at times ambiguously so. People are rediscovering that the life of prayer requires conditions for a life of prayer, and that these conditions create a harmony, an equilibrium of life. Christian prayer may create this harmony, but this doesn't make it an exercise of wisdom. The Christian prays to God for God's sake, because God alone is enough. He worships.

The Christian is not spiritualist, he is spiritual. He seeks a remote God who became our neighbor. A God who makes us measure his distance as we draw near. Today more than ever before, human prayer is a prayer in tension, a prayer of man respectful of an inaccessible God. A prayer of man in love with a nearby God. The paradox of Christian prayer is here: in addressing the transcendent God, it never materializes man's relationship to God. In addressing a transcendent Creator God, prayer incarnates man's relationship to God, which is always spiritual:

Lord, God of down here, God of over there
You call us and you remain unperceived
Hidden God—manifested God
You are the Eternal of today
But what would your eternity be
—that essential beyondness—
if everything beyond the sky
were only oblivion
of what's down here on earth?
Don't look down at us from up there!
We strive to live now
what we will live tomorrow
for the centuries of centuries.

· Prayer to a God Who Made Himself Human

The way you address God shapes his face: "Tell me what God you pray to, and I'll tell you who your God is." The wager of prayer is God himself. "Tell me how you pray, and I'll tell you who you are." The wager of prayer is man, in the image of God. "Tell me how the congregation prays, and I'll tell you which is your Church." The wager of prayer is Christ's body.

Not a God Who Makes Us Pray
—Not Words, but a WORD

Our God is not a God who makes us pray, but a God we pray to. I mean a God we love. He's not a Boss God whom we give business presents to. As Amos says: "He hates our holocausts, our oblations, our sacrifices" (Amos 5:21 –24). God waits for us to pray because that's his way of showing us his affection. But how can we find the right words? Words? Not words but a Word. Prayer is essentially God's Word in the heart of man's words. Prayer is a gift of the Word. It is not an obligation that man must fulfill to satisfy God, to satisfy his wishes. It is not even an initiative by man, who gives himself the joy of addressing God. No; prayer is the acceptance of God's gift to mankind, the power of speaking through the Word, which is God's own Son, He who teaches us to be the Word for God. Through God, man becomes gifted to speak to God.

Let's rediscover this Word of origin if we wish to restore to prayer the grace that is man's encounter with God in his mystery.

Let's rediscover the Speech/Word if we wish to avoid being misled by the present-day renewal of liturgical language to the vulgar impasses of chitchat.

So, let's repeat it: not words, but a Word. A word carrying those of today's words that are the effective signs of the Reality of the Word Made Flesh in our world. A Word that manifests not only the love that God brings mankind and the love that mankind brings back to him, but also the love that man can bring to himself.

—Not Titles, but His Name . . .

In prayer, the man of our century needs to find God in the fullness of God as much as he needs to find himself fully in this quest. Yes, man needs to find himself as he is, without even knowing who he is. Find himself in the night with its nightmares and in the day with its daydreams. Similarly, he needs to find himself other than he is in this striving to become himself; to become what God summons him to become.

In this desire for God's fullness, the secularized Christian can no longer endure the human definitions of God; because, if man sequesters God in titles, representations that caricature him, he is only imprisoning himself and hurting himself. Our transcendent God is not an official God, petrified in the ready-made formulas with which we have to address him. Our creator God is not a superman God of the universe who has to be overwhelmed with cosmetic compliments. The prayer of praise is not flattery. Our God who became human is no humanitarianist God. Our brotherly God is no buddy-buddy God. Our seductive God is no Jesus Christ Superstar. Our revealed God—revealed without exhausting the mystery—remains the Unknowable, the Ineffable. The Completely Other. We don't know Who He is. We don't know who we are. So then what's so amazing about not finding words? We can only stammer: "How beautiful our God is!" Saying that someone is beautiful is quite a lot. Saying to someone "You're beautiful" is saying "I love you." God's beauty is the name we give to his love which calls us in tenderness. Our God is the God of tenderness.

> Trinity God
> we repeat that you are
> Great. The greatest. Infinite.
> We proclaim your glory.
> We speak to you about grace and freedom.
> Who will speak to you about beauty?
> You are beautiful, Lord.
> Like a breath of air,
> your tenderness is imperceptible.
> Like the sea wind,
> the breath of your love is irresistible.
> But you attract
> only those who want to follow you.
> You seduce
> only those who let themselves be loved.
> From the depth of our hearts or the tips
> of our tongues,
> however we can,
> we say to you:
> "I love you."

A Theoretical God?
—Negotiating His Distress

To love the fact that God is beautiful doesn't mean that the God of Christians is a luxury God for ethereal lovers of beauty. Modern man's concern for truth is expressed in committed prayer. The Christian no longer wishes to speak to a theoretical God, a God to whom one keeps repeating the same phrases, come what may. One can't, for instance, say to God that he's good, as though nothing were wrong—because in everyday life, absurdity flays you and human rebellion broods latently in suffering and the outrage against evil. Man needs to negotiate his distress, to speak and to speak to himself. At bottom, he is not questioning God's goodness, but since life is opaque, man can't always recognize God's goodness. And if he doubts, he doubts himself as well as God. "I no longer know what I know," said Saint John of the Cross. Yes, in prayer, we unlearn whatever we think we know about life; for life with God always teaches you something else. We renounce our property. We become true. Prayer gives astonishing lucidity, the lucidity of humility which is called truth. This is why today's man rejects the formalism in which we participate by saying what is expected of us. The priest himself doesn't escape this unbearable feeling of sometimes reciting things on command, spouting clichés that cannot take into account every person he knows in the congregation, coming out with stereotypes that sometimes go against certain people. Today's man has many failings. But we can't accuse him of insincerity.... He is unable to act "as if." Thus, after the tragic death of a twenty-year-old stupidly killed in an accident, prayer can legitimately express the agitation of the human heart and go along with the Psalmist's cry, the cry of all those who lash out against God in the Bible. With them, we say: "Lord, you reveal yourself to be the just and good God, you tell us that you are Life, that you love life, that you give life; well, look at how this young person has just been robbed of life. Do you realize what we are feeling? How does that affect you?"

—*Prayer, an Act of Faith*

It is an act of faith to present oneself to God as we are, crying out our distress, our passion. God is not above this. He has gone to the heart of all of our passions. God, the passionate incarnate in Jesus Christ. To believe is to consume one's faith in the fire that is prayer! It is the cry within us of the absolute desire for God. The cry of the Spirit calling: "Father!" The cry of the apostles to Christ: "Teach us how to pray." And if we couldn't say everything to God, tell me to whom we *could* say it? Jesus is someone to speak to. Always.

Jesus is he to whom one can state one's disbelief: "Lord, I believe, help my unbelief!" (Mark 9:24). No one is a total believer. Prayer evangelizes us: it reveals whatever disbelief we may have. That's why we have to keep prayer Christian, that is, we must not empty it of its specifically Christian content, nor reduce it to the demands of a generous man addressing a humanitarian God. The more we heed the secularized person, the more we have to respect the specific nature of Christian prayer, a prayer that addresses the Father, the Son, the Spirit. The prayer of Jesus himself who takes us into the mystery of his death and resurrection. The prayer of the Spirit in our hearts. The prayer of the Church making the Word a reality.

> "Blessed Trinity!
> you're not the God of philosophers....
> Like the sea abandoning itself on the shore
> in a long parley with the sand,

I won't stop the motion
of the eternal desire
of my heart:
You are He whom my heart seeks:
You the Unique! Father-Son-Spirit
Singular Plural. . . .
for the centuries of centuries!"

The Deceased Christian of Christianity
—The Intelligence of Common Prayer

Today, it seems urgent to rediscover freedom of expression, a devouring fire and genuine frankness in the liturgy. However, we must understand that we don't speak to God in a congregation the way we speak to him in the privacy of our hearts. In a congregation a certain priestly formula is imposed. To have words of common prayer makes sense. Thus, the celebrant mustn't impose his slogans and his subjectivity. The Roman liturgy has the genius of objectivity that respects others, but it doesn't always avoid the pitfall of coldness. How can it get out of its world, out of its stereotype vocabulary today? How can it bring out the mental patterns underlying the language that grows more and more alien to us? For that's what it's all about: outlook. The outlook of the secularized Christian is diametrically opposed to the outlook of the Christian of Christianity.

When the Christian was immersed in an agrarian and Christian civilization, he felt at ease in the waters of this world, with which he was familiar. Today, in a technological civilization that is urban and dechristianized, the Christian is losing his foothold. If we do not share the sensibility of the secularized man who feels lost in the Church, if we do not have the missionary concern for trying to make faith relate to people who are in tune with today's world, then, obviously, we can't understand this perspective. One might very easily regard this cultural revolution as an historical accident; but in fact, it's a turning point, an irreversible change.

—Each Culture Has Its Sensibility . . .
The critical point for the Church is to succeed in changing her outlook. For centuries, the Church managed to impose a common language. Yet today, it can be universal only by empathizing with every type of outlook, respecting every culture, being in tune with every sensibility. All of which can raise a lot of questions within every congregation, indeed, all Christian congregations throughout the world. The unity of the liturgy can no longer exist on a uniform level. It must be achieved in diversity. But how can we retranslate into multiple languages the traditional terms belonging to the treasury of the revelation without betraying the doctrinal content. This is the question we ask in regard to certain words such as *Almighty*, *Mercy*, etc.

The title of *Almighty* for God is found throughout the Bible. Today, it is construed with all the overtones that this adjective can have in the modern world. Might is the strength to strike, the power of the stronger. *Might* or *power*, according to the secular connotation, is the opposite of the Poverty of the beatitudes. When we speak of God's might we mean the power of the Gospel. How can we express it? "Lord, you whose only power is that of love. . . ." If we can't find equivalents, explanations that restore full vigor to ligurgical words, we may easily turn the modern language of liturgy into a new dead tongue.

Mercy—this word goes against the grain of modern sensibilities. It is still impregnated, as in the story of the blind man of Jericho, with the disparagement articulated by Nietzsche, who regards mercy as unbearable condescension. Perhaps all we need do is quite simply justify the use of this essential Biblical word, which expresses the infinite love of God, who can do everything when a human being can do nothing more. We could try paraphrases such as: "Lord, take me into your love." Or we could enhance the value of the word by explaining it without really seeming to explain it. . . .

> If Mercy
> is the face of your Love
> which takes men's misery to heart
> then we can say:
> > Lord, have mercy.
>
> If Mercy
> lets Hope pierce
> the heart of despair
> then we can say:
> > Lord, have mercy.
>
> If Mercy
> is the power of your Love
> which can do anything
> in Him who makes us strong
> then we can say:
> > Lord, have mercy.

—*A True Prayer*

In trying to express his feelings, the secularized Chrisian agrees to be poor in his prayer. His prayer is a quest for God. It joins together all people who don't know, who don't realize; who don't know that one can seek, who don't know that one can find, who don't know Him who is unknown and yet who reveals himself, giving us this mad hope: "Some day, I'll see him the way I'm seen, I'll love him the way he loves me!"

But how can I say to God in all truth that I love him infinitely, if infinity escapes me?

Poetry, the Inner Kingdom
—A Space of Freedom

Poetry isn't well liked. Too often, it's judged according to its by-products. A world of artificial blue flowers. And the poet himself is often pictured as a bearded eccentric. And besides, you will say, poetry isn't accessible to everyone. If it's true that every person is like Molière's Monsieur Jourdain, who's been speaking prose all his life without realizing it, then everybody is a poet without realizing it. Just as one can like music without being able to read it, so too one can enter the poetic universe without knowing what a verse is. Poetry, while presupposing a certain charisma, is not primarily a technique; it's an inward movement, a spiritual quality, an openness to freedom. That's why it's an accomplice of prayer. If you reject poetry, the inner kingdom, I don't see how you can admit prayer, God's kingdom of dawn. Poetry is a space of freedom. The goal of poetry is not so much to find explicitly poetic expressions, a marked-out literary form, as to bring out an existential background that evokes impressions which grant the hearer the grace of saying to himself that which is beyond words. In a liturgical congregation, every participant must, within the celebrant's words, be able to say in his own way what he hears uttered on his behalf. Yes, in the silence of his heart, in tune with the silence of all other hearts, the participant must have inward understanding to retranslate what he hears proclaimed by the celebrant. If the Christian in a congregation doesn't activate the celebrant's words, it's because the Church is losing the power of speech in its ministers.

—The Universal in Every Man

Poetic language is the language of fire that the Spirit invents for every human being, letting everyone understand the wonders of God in his own language. Poetic language respects the uniqueness of each person in relation to the congregation, for it only suggests. It's not a conceptual language that necessarily imposes ideas; it's a language that makes images. It pulverizes words. It makes anything limited in a concept explode. It makes a light burst from beyond. It creates á new world. Each person has his field of stars. It allows us to find, at the fine point of the soul, the invulnerable source of living water. It avoids getting anecdotal. It doesn't bog down in particular examples that leave out people who can't recognize themselves in the details. Poetic language has no frontiers. It reaches the whole world; the world which we each carry within ourselves. Existentially, it joins with whatever is universal in every person. Those who, in the name of realism, transform prayers of universal meaning into moralizing examinations of life are exploiting prayers as carriers of their own ideas or lack of ideas. Prayer must be courageously committed on the level of events, for the point is not to flee the topical; and likewise, it must be disengaged from narratives of newsy items, from group or movement slogans. Committed prayer doesn't mean prayer marked by positions or bludgeoning opinions. Prayer remains free. We are not to dictate what God should do. All the heavy "so thats" in our universal prayers, dragging whole sentences of typically Christian phraseology, aptly translate the impotence of our insipid chitchat.

—As in the Language of Love

Poetic language reveals that praying is not so much saying words as letting oneself be seized by the Word. The Word is all-encompassing. Praying is not so much understanding as letting oneself be understood by Him who understands everything. One loves before understanding, one understands only because one loves. In prayer, we become the other, even if the intellectual content of prayer often eludes us. I become God's, as, in the language of love, I become the person I love. Language invites each person to go into himself—a fundamental act if one wishes to get out of oneself. Present to others as much as to myself, I stop talking about myself. Now that I'm receptive to the other, my prayer becomes a prayer of others. A prayer of God's. I catch myself letting God speak. I catch myself letting others speak. In prayer, God and others speak through me. I am their voice.

The Distraction of God

How can we ask God to carry the world that we carry in ourselves, this invisible world? We mustn't think that a prayer of asking should obligatorily be translated into

explicit formulations, precise petitions. To ask is not to de-
mand. To ask is sometimes merely to tell God what's in our
hearts. Likewise, to thank God isn't necessarily to speak
prefaces and gush out litanies of gratitude. Saying thank-
you may be allowing the inspiration of joy to flower within
us, allowing the fantasies of the Spirit to overcome us and
help us discover the most original things in the most banal
things. Ultimately, each individual must invent his own
form of prayer. Each person is unique, and thus finds his
unique way of saying what everyone says.... Why have
human respect for yourself and then regard yourself as ri-
diculous because, like the Juggler of Notre Dame, you make
unexpected words dance? We have to be humble. A community that refuses to learn how to pray through its members as they are is a rigid community. To pray is always to
learn how to pray, hence, to admit that none of us succeeds
in praying. If there were less regard for dignity, we would
pray better in Church, with our children, with our friends.

But, we've talked enough. Let me try to do what I have
been saying.

Here is a prayer that hasn't been fussed over. It is what it
is. It's a prayer in a subway. Prayer doesn't stop because you
start ad-libbing a story. We offer to God any distractions
we may have. Prayer is the finest distraction. The distraction of God.

<pre>
God   God   God   God
God
I
God
You
God
</pre>

nothing else
Everyone else
My God
Our God
God of many
God of some
God now
Maintaining existence
Existence to live
To live on Saturday night
The subway's noisy on Saturday night
It's not like other days when tomorrow's Sunday
People talk loudly. People laugh. Their clothes smell clean.
On Monday morning, the subway is suffocating.
Not a word. To each his own.

Lord
You are the God of the week
God of weekends
God of Sundays
God of holidays.
The subway runs on Sundays and holidays.
And they run too
the people who run the stations
the people who run the trains
supervisors
assistant supervisors
and all those who aren't supervisors
and you Lord, whom I celebrated in the hymns
    when I was a child:
"You're our supervisor on earth!"

God   God   God   God
Systolic motion of axles
in me your name like a stake
God adored
God love

God light
God Father
God Son
God Spirit
God hammered in my heart
my eyes closed.
My eyes can't help recognizing
in all those eyes with dark circles
God weary on weary faces.

God I am changing
When will I be new?
God you never change
You are always New.
God of our stations
God of my road
God, come down from my cross
God, don't abandon me
God, it's me, open up to me!
God You're great
I'd like to call you
God my little one
God tell me
no one's ever told me
what comes after the last stop
God where does the subway go after that?
God where does the darkness go?

This darkness isn't pessimism. Or fear. The darkness is
the color of hope for those in the tunnel. Darkness merely
suggests that all praying expresses the passage from shadow
to light. It was dark when Jesus gave up the Spirit. All
prayer is paschal. Prayer makes us die to ourselves so that
we may rise again.

• The Eucharist, the First and Last Word of Prayer

A prayer that doesn't have the weight of the cross has no weight. The weight of the resurrection is the weight of the cross. The prayer of the Christian is always the prayer of Christ dead and resurrected, reexperiencing perfectly what every Christian stammers. Christ's manner of praying today in each one of us, realizing that which we tend towards, is known as the Eucharist.

Human prayer, God's prayer, universal prayer—the Eucharist is the totalizing dimension of Christian life. The Eucharist is prayer moving towards infinity. It communicates the denseness of the Spirit to all fibers of my life. It extends the power of the resurrection to the entire world that I carry inside me. By saying thank-you in communion to the risen Christ, I join all those I love on earth as in heaven, I join all those I name throughout the universe. God, whom I join, join in me that which I hope, the hope of the world: Peace. Justice. Love. Truth. Light. Joy. These aren't just my aims, these are God's aim for the world. Thus, the Eucharist lets me assimilate within myself the taste of God that prayer sometimes has so much trouble expressing:

> God
> This word can't do anymore
> than say what you are not.
> This word is bursting to say
> what you are:
> God
>
> Here is the Bread
> It is your Word
> It speaks of your life.

> Here is the Wine
> It is your Life
> Our Eucharist life.

Thus, because God has given us the Eucharist in the heart of our lives, we can say: I'm hungry for God. The Eucharist, the Bread of life, expresses well our need for food: being regenerated, completed by someone else. The body, in its need for food, admits it is unable to live without the strength that comes from beyond itself. In the moment of communion, the person who stretches out his hand to receive the bread recognizes that he is nothing without Him who is Life. The Eucharist is the poetry of God: it tells us through this bread what God does with us in his hand.

> God
> Here is the Bread
> It speaks about You
> better than any life
> here is the Eucharist.

> God
> Here is the Wine
> It sings
> better than any vintage
> It sings of your vine
> better than any praises
> here is the Eucharist

Alpha and Omega, the Eucharist, the heart of faith, is the first and last word of prayer. Isn't this yearning, joined to what Valéry Larbaud suggests to us, in a different context, the epigraph of this book:

> "Perhaps I hunger for things unknown."